Praise 1

"Celeste is about resilience. I've had the privilege of knowing Celeste for over twenty years and her service to others in need is legendary. And now with *Garbage Bag Girl* her work will not only encourage but help others find their voice."

– DAVE PELZER

1 International bestselling author of *A Child called 'It'*; National Jefferson Award recipient; Author of *Return to the River*

"*Garbage Bag Girl* is a raw narrative about not only what it is like to experience abuse and neglect, but to subsequently be parented by a well intentioned child welfare system that struggles to be genuinely child centered, family driven, and healing centered.

Celeste Edmunds is a profile in courage and resiliency. Her lived child welfare experience serves as a testament to the importance of loving family connections for every child and of the complicated, but very real need a child has to be connected to who they are and where they came from. With grace and compassion, Celeste has taken her own difficult experiences and channeled them for decades into bettering the lives of other children and families. She is a gift.

– DIANE MOORE

Former Director of Utah's Division of Child and Family Services

GARBAGE BAG *Girl*

GARBAGE BAG *Girl*

CELESTE L. EDMUNDS
AND RICHARD PAUL EVANS

ASCENDT PUBLISHING

Garbage Bag Girl
Copyright © 2023 by Celeste Edmunds and Richard Paul Evans

First Ascendt trade paperback edition November 2023

Ascendt Publishing and colophon are trademarks of Ascendt Publishing LLC.

For information about special discounts for bulk purchases
please contact Ascendt Publishing at (801) 870-3925

For speaking events, please text or call Diane Glad at (801) 870-3925

Cover designed by Aksaramantra Design
Designed using assets from Freepik.com
Interior design by: Francine Platt of Eden Graphics, Inc.

Paperback ISBN 978-1-958626-63-4
eBook ISBN 978-1-958626-64-1
Audio ISBN 978-1-958626-65-8

The Library of Congress has cataloged this edition as follows:
2023920842

Edmunds, Celeste, Evans, Richard Paul.
Garbage Bag Girl:
1st Ascendt Trade Paperback edition

1 3 5 7 9 10 8 6 4 2

To my mom, Carlie.
Thank you for truly giving me life.
Celeste L. Edmunds

To the unseen children everywhere.
Richard Paul Evans

ACKNOWLEDGMENTS

THANK YOU TO MY MOM, CARLIE. Thank you does not accurately express my appreciation to you. Without you, I would not be here. To Debbie Rasmussen, Francine Platt, and Diane Glad, thank you for your time and heart in putting my story on paper. To Rick (you know him as Richard Paul) Evans, for your years of love, friendship, and mentoring. The vital work we get to do together would not be possible without your heart, faith, and courage. To Keri Evans, our backbone, and my beautiful friend, I love you. To my kids, Eric, Alex "Eddie," Mykaella, bonus daughter Allie, and grandson Matthias, thank you for your love and support and for teaching me how to love. To my sister Tawny, I'd still give my life for you. To Kent, Sylvia, Tyler, and Lisa, thank you for showing me what 'home' looks like. To Tammy, my BFF, you're behind the scenes; never-ending love and support are always present and felt. To my CBI family, Kristin, Julia, Bridgett, Barry, and Katie, your strength and encouragement are so valued. I am grateful to be on this journey to serve God's children with you. Jenn, thank you for saving my life. Without you, there wouldn't be a story to tell. To Shane, thank you for coming back for me. And to the rest of my tribe: my Gen-shai family, my San Francisco Johnson family, Carlos & Emily, Tami, Tonia, Raymond, Krista, Amy & my Yogi family, Alan & Susan, Lynn, and Vinney, thank you for showing up for me and reminding me that I am capable of doing important and hard things, even when I am unsure of myself.

– CELESTE L. EDMUNDS

The authors would like to especially thank author Deborah Rasmussen for her help in researching and developing this book.

AUTHORS' NOTE

This book contains graphic content. Out of respect
for truth and the child who suffered the injustices
sited in this book, the authors chose to describe
those experiences just as they happened.

Celeste L. Edmunds and Richard Paul Evans

Foreword

By Richard Paul Evans

*I*N THE SUMMER OF 1874, Mary Ellen Wilson, a nine-year-old girl from New York City, made national news. Incredibly, the event that sparked a media frenzy over the child wouldn't warrant a mention in a newspaper today: Mary Ellen was abused by her parents.

The abuse was of such severity that the child likely would have died if she hadn't been rescued by Etta Wheeler, a Methodist Missionary working in the girl's neighborhood.

Ms. Wheeler's initial efforts to help Mary Ellen were fruitless. No one wanted to believe that child abuse existed–or even that it *could* exist. And even if it did, there were no laws on the books prohibiting cruelty to children.

There *were,* however, laws prohibiting cruelty to animals. After repeated failures in her efforts to seek justice for the child, the determined Wheeler took her case to Henry Bergh, the founder of the American Society for the Prevention of Cruelty to Animals (ASPCA). Bergh and his organization won protection for Mary Ellen by arguing that a child was, in fact, a member of the animal kingdom, worthy of the same protection under law *as a dog*.

Despite the national outrage over the case, the commotion quickly died down leaving little changed. Society once again closed its eyes to child abuse.

Shortly after the turn of the century, public recognition of child abuse faced another setback when renowned psychologist Sigmund Freud publicly theorized that his patients' claims of childhood sexual abuse were merely repressed fantasies.

It wasn't until the early nineteen-sixties, *nearly a century* after the Wilson case, that the medical profession formally *agreed* upon the existence of child abuse and laws protecting children began to be written.

Despite that progress, still today, hundreds of thousands of children around the world carry the emotional and physical scars of abuse. *Garbage Bag Girl* is the story of one of those children.

The first time I met Celeste she was working across the hall from me in an office building in downtown Salt Lake City. At the time I was a partner in a small advertising agency. I had just written my first book, *The Christmas Box*, which had become a national bestseller. As fan mail and the pressures of writing my next book mounted, I realized the need for a personal assistant. Peculiarly, just a few hours later, Celeste walked into my office looking for a job. I hired her.

In the words of Humphrey Bogart, *it was the beginning of a beautiful friendship*. As we worked closely together, Celeste would occasionally drop hints about her childhood. All of it got my attention. In fact, one incident she shared went on to inspire my bestselling novel, *Finding Noel*.

As I learned more about Celeste's childhood, I encouraged her to write her story in its entirety. *Garbage Bag Girl* is that story—the account of one girl's resilience in the face of heartbreak, neglect, and uncertainty. Perhaps, even more remarkable than her story itself, is the fact that Celeste found the courage and vulnerability to share it. Incredibly, despite the darkness of her journey, Celeste's story remains one of forgiveness, hope and inspiration.

I believe that *Garbage Bag Girl* should be required reading for every parent, foster parent, child welfare worker, and schoolteacher; in short, everyone who advocates and cares for the children of the world.

Prologue

O N PAPER, I DON'T EXIST. I mean, I have a birth certificate and social security number, but the state records of the years my story took place have all been destroyed. Back then, child welfare records were kept on paper in alphabetized manilla folders in steel file cabinets or some back room with copious rows of banker boxes. They were stored for ten years then shredded or burned or whatever they do with such information. When I went to child services to see my records, there was nothing left for me. I wish my memories could be so easily expunged.

I suppose that children never really know how screwed up their lives are until they are somehow rescued from them. Of course, they don't. It's all they know. This is the story of my childhood. Until now, it has existed as a shadow in my head—a searing collection of incidents, occurrences, lessons, pain, and heartache sprinkled with too few fleeting moments of hope and happiness. On occasion, I have shared bits and pieces of my childhood, but this time, as painful as it turned out to be, I wanted to get it all out of my head. Most importantly, I want others to understand who I am. Or *we* are. As I wrote down my experiences, I realized that my story wasn't just about me. It's about all of us who were raised in the child welfare system. Hopefully it will help someone. Freeing that broken little girl out of my psyche has already helped me.

As difficult as much of it is to read (and for me to write), in the end, this is my story about hope.

PART 1

CHAPTER ONE

Who's the Mother?

*L*EO TOLSTOY WROTE, "Happy families are all alike; every unhappy family is unhappy in its own way." I suppose that's true of mine. I was born in the town of West Valley City, Utah, a suburb of Salt Lake City. My parents were

Lynn and Veda Anderson. I had one younger sister, Tawny, and a little brother, Austin.

We lived a nomadic childhood, and I don't remember staying anywhere longer than six months. Whenever we found a place, it was only a matter of time before we were evicted, which left us temporarily in a motel or staying with other family members.

I remember my mother spending most of her time on the couch sleeping. I was two years older than Tawny, and my "mother" duties began for me at around the age of seven. At first, I would ask Mom if I could help, usually when Tawny or I were hungry, but she'd usually just get mad at me for waking her up, so I eventually stopped asking for permission and just fulfilled my mother's duties—at least as well as a seven-year-old could. I knew how to boil water, and we seemed to always have macaroni and cheese in the house. I had seen Mom make it before, and, standing on a stool at the stove, it was something I could do. Tawny and I both loved it, and if we were lucky enough to have hot dogs, I would slice them into small coins and add them to the macaroni. The hot dogs were a delicacy.

Austin was seven years younger than me, and he needed me, too. I figured out how to hold his bottle exactly right so he could drink and fall asleep. It seemed like he always had stomach aches; I learned later that this was because he was born addicted to drugs. I remember vividly when my sister and I snuck into the hospital's NICU to see him in his incubator—a tiny baby attached to beeping machines and tubes to feed and help him breathe. We watched his chest rise and fall each time he gasped for air. He barely survived. His middle initial was T for Tuffy.

The only time I felt like I could be a child was when I stayed with my cousins at my favorite relatives' houses, Aunt Ann and Uncle Greg or Aunt May and Uncle Gary. They had beautiful, well-kept homes with manicured lawns and shrubs and backyards with trees to climb. Some of my fondest memories were of us playing at their houses. Especially climbing their trees. I loved to climb trees and still do.

Aunt Ann told me that Mom, Dad, and I lived with my dad's parents until I was eighteen months old. Even though she was just in high school, she used to get up with me in the middle of the night, feed me, and take me with her to some of the places she went. She also has fond memories of those times. I visited with her when I started writing this book. She cried as she told me she had always felt guilty for not taking me when I was put up for adoption at eight years old. I cried, too. My life would have been a very different story. This book wouldn't be necessary. Still, I was able to thank her for all she had done for me. It was a healing conversation we both needed after forty-one years. It also helped me to realize that through my relationship with her, I had learned to feel, to connect, and to love.

My dad was an aspiring guitar player. He was playing one of his gigs at a local bar when he met my mom. She was just nineteen. Three weeks later, they were married at my grandparents' home, and nine months later, I was born. They named me Celeste. I was told it meant "heavenly."

My father was always in pain. He was diagnosed with polio at birth and suffered through twelve years of reconstructive surgeries. He was born before the polio vaccination was available, so he was heavily medicated from the start to manage the pain, setting him firmly on the path of addiction. I don't think he and, by association, the rest of us ever had a chance for a normal life. The culmination of my parents' pain, compounded with their addictions and an unexpected marriage and child, was a perfect storm that started us down a difficult path to an uncertain end.

Though I remember my father as being loving and caring, my mother spoke of him as being cruel and abusive. It was Aunt Ann who told me about how much fun he was when he was younger. Their entire family had a natural gift for music, and Dad played a "mean" guitar. All eight of the siblings played musical instruments, so music was always a part of their family gatherings. I, too, inherited this musical gift. It sometimes brought me joy but at other times, pain and humiliation.

As I wrote earlier, I don't have many memories of "being a kid." Since I was caring for my siblings, I never had that luxury. I was always worried about adult things—where we were going to sleep at night, when my parents would fight next, or if the police would knock on our door looking for my dad. I worried about strange men coming to deliver "product" to my mom in exchange for sex, and, if she was unavailable, whether or not I would be expected to provide payment.

My relationship with my mom was always unhealthy, though I could never fully understand why. It was like we were always in competition over who was in charge. After all, I did more to care for Tawny and Austin than she did. And though it was necessary, and I thought she should have been grateful, she often looked at me with spite in her eyes as if my very being reminded her of her failure. But I also felt something else, something deeper. I think she believed I stood in the way of her relationship with her husband. That's the way I felt, anyway.

After I decided to write this book, I talked to my biological mother about the past. In doing so, I learned for fact what I had always believed—that my mother had never really loved herself. I suppose it was one of the few things that we really had in common. Neither of us grew up feeling like we were anything special or of value to anyone. Mom described her own mother as being emotionally unavailable to her, always in unhealthy relationships, with an abusive boyfriend that lived with them for years. From my perspective, it felt like she was describing herself.

My mom never knew her dad, but an uncle who lived with them sexually abused her for years. When she was fifteen, she was coming home from a party when she was raped by two boys her same age. Her mother did not believe that any of this had happened, confirming my mom's belief that she could trust no one—especially men.

When I was twenty years old, I went in search of my parents and located the adoption agency where I was adopted into the Hatt family. It was there I came upon a psychological report that was written about my mom when she was in a drug rehabilitation center. The report stated that my mother's mental capacity had stopped developing at age fifteen. She could not move forward mentally or developmentally, making it impossible for her to take care of herself, much less raise a family.

When I look back at the whole picture—my mother trapped in the mentality of a fifteen-year-old and my dad, just twenty-three, a drug addict with no real job skills—it had to be nearly impossible for them to provide a secure environment for raising children. It was a perfect recipe for child abuse at every level.

CHAPTER TWO

Silent Night, Holy Night

WHEREVER WE LIVED, Mom kept a belt hanging on the wall. This was to appear intimidating and to keep us in line. When we played too loud and woke her up, she would struggle to get off the couch, threaten us with the belt, get something to eat, and then collapse back onto the couch.

I loved Tawny from the moment she was born and felt a maternal need to take care of her. Even as I held her in the hospital, I knew it was up to me to keep her safe. I spent nearly every minute I could with her when she was little. When she was five, I began taking her to and from kindergarten. We would hold hands while we walked. Looking back, I realize that I never felt like her sister, but her mom. That would prove unhealthy. Children aren't capable of raising children. Nor should they be.

Taking care of Tawny, I felt like I had purpose and

meaning. When our mother wasn't on the couch, she and I fought. Our days were chaotic since I was usually the one in charge and felt that I knew better than Mom what my brother and sister needed.

I don't remember my brother being home as much as Tawny and I were. I later learned that he often stayed with family members. We never had a chance to bond as young children and so never formed a long-term relationship—even as adults.

My sister and I went to the same elementary school, so I knew my way around the place. Most days I would drop her off at class, always smiling at her teacher, hoping she would see how grown-up I was and be proud of me. I went to my classroom happy that we would both have a good meal because we were having school lunch that day.

I usually didn't play with kids at recess. Instead, I watched through the chain-link fence that divided our grade areas while Tawny played. I wanted to make sure she was safe. Happily, the kids in her class loved her, and she had lots of friends. She was smart, funny, kind, and her hair looked so pretty the way it naturally fell into little curls along the bottom. She was all girl.

On the other hand, I was not blessed with cute hair or a cute girl shape of any kind. I was tall and lanky; my hair was straight and stuck to my head like a helmet. I felt like I looked more like a boy than a girl. I was also more comfortable hanging out with boys than girls. Most of the girls my age wore cute outfits with pretty hair bows, and they giggled a lot. They seemed to talk only about each other. I had no interest in any of that, so I stayed away from them.

School ended at 2:30, and Tawny and I had an arrangement that she would not leave her classroom until I picked her up. If our mom was not there to meet us, I would lie and tell the teacher that Mom was waiting in the car, and we needed to hurry, or she would be late for work. The teacher likely knew we didn't have a car and I was lying, but I'm guessing that my consistency made her feel comfortable, and she always let Tawny leave with me.

We typically got home by 3:00. We usually shared a snack I saved from lunch, and then I helped her with her letters, numbers, and colors—things I had already learned. I didn't feel like it was safe to leave her alone while I took a bath, so we bathed together. It gave us time to play with toys, and we used the shampoo for bubbles—we weren't supposed to, but we did anyway. It was simple and fun, and we were rarely interrupted, so it became a routine part of our day.

After bath time, I combed her hair, and, no matter the month, I sang her favorite song, "Silent Night." Afterward, I read her a bedtime story and tucked her into bed. She almost always asked for another song and a second story, but I said no because I had to do my homework.

This particular day, right after Tawny went to bed, Dad came home drunk and started screaming at Mom for cheating on him. Even as a kid, I was not sure when he thought this could have happened because she was rarely off the couch, but he insisted. They continued to argue long into the night.

"You're drunk!" my mother shouted. "You know damn well I haven't cheated on you! How do I know you haven't cheated on me? You're never here, and when you are, all you do is yell at me."

"I know you have men in and out of the house! You're here all day while the girls are in school, and you never take care of our son—we have to pawn him off on family because you're so strung out all the time. What kind of a mother are you?"

"I could ask the same questions of you!"

Their screaming went back and forth for what felt like hours; then, I heard a loud crash. It woke Tawny, and she started to cry. I told her to hide under the blankets while I checked on Mom. When I went into the living room, Mom was crying. I asked Dad to stop yelling at her, but he wouldn't listen. I screamed at him from the top of my lungs.

"Daddy! Please stop yelling at Mom!"

"Shut up, Celeste!"

"I won't shut up until you stop yelling at Mom!"

I was taken completely by surprise when I was hurled across the coffee table. My dad had *never* hurt me before. I hit the table so hard that the glass broke. A sharp pain shot through my leg as my head hit the floor. Both of my parents hurried to my side as I tried to stand up. An enormous piece of glass was poking out of my leg, and blood was streaming down the side of my thigh.

They both started to cry, and Dad tried to tell me he was

sorry, and he would never hurt his baby girl. Between the two of them, they pulled the glass out, put hydrogen peroxide on the wound, and wrapped it in some sort of gauze.

My head was spinning, but I didn't cry. I never let them see me cry because that was all I had that was mine that I felt in control of. When they stopped fussing over me, I went back to our room to check on Tawny.

"Sissy sad?" she asked.

"Sissy isn't sad."

"Sissy, okay?"

"Sissy's okay."

Tawny and I had a game we played when things got bad. She liked to go inside a closet and pretend we were driving away. We would make loud noises as though we were shifting gears. I guess this helped us feel in control. But not tonight. Tonight, she and I slept on a mattress on the floor. She snuggled up next to me, and I sang "Silent Night" until she fell asleep. I remember feeling so grateful that she was safe and had not seen what had happened in the living room.

My head throbbed from hitting the floor, but I finally fell asleep, anticipating what I knew the next morning would be like. Mom always did the same thing when she felt guilty that she hadn't taken care of us.

Just as I predicted, we woke the next day with our clothes laid out and the smell of breakfast cooking. It was rare that she cooked, so I figured she was extra happy. This was a special day as scrambled eggs were on the menu.

We must have gotten food from the local food pantry or a family member, or maybe Mom had gotten some money from Dad that he earned from the gig the night before. He was in his thirties now, but he still played guitar at bars when he wasn't in jail or drug rehab.

It was unusual that Mom was so happy, and it made me angry that she only acted like a real mother after a traumatic experience. Still, I tried to enjoy the peculiarity of no chaos.

Despite the yelling and occasional violence, I loved my dad and considered myself a daddy's girl. When he was sober, he was happy and fun. After nights of him and Mom yelling and screaming, or after he had been gone for extended periods of time (usually jail), he would sober up for a few weeks, and those times were filled with lots of talk, hugs, and baseball. I loved to go to baseball games with my dad even more than I loved climbing trees.

Dad's biological family loved to spend time together, and I was close to my uncles, aunts, and cousins on his side of the family. When our family was in a rare healthy place, we spent time with them playing baseball or listening to my dad and his siblings sing and play music. I thought they were all fantastically talented, and I loved being with them.

Mom, on the other hand, was always difficult for me to be around. She seemed to always be depressed and mad at Dad or us for something. I remember wondering if maybe Dad didn't come home because of her.

Now, as an adult, I know it was not her fault that he was

not around much. Dad was a different person with Mom than he was with me. It's sad, but the reality is my parents were an unhealthy, addicted couple with three children, no money, and more complications than I could begin to understand as a child.

Still, through our strained existence and dysfunction, Dad always had hugs for Tawny and me. But there would come a time when those hugs would turn into distant memories that would hold a place in my heart for the rest of my life.

CHAPTER THREE

Paying Mom's Debt

WHEN MY DAD WASN'T AROUND, I didn't feel safe. Especially because people, mostly men, were always stopping by the house to drop "things" off. Sometimes, a family member or the local church would bring us food. Other times, we would stand in line at the local food bank hoping we would get something special, like bacon.

But other times, like this day, "Dad's friends," as Mom would call them, would stop by. It was my mom's way of compartmentalizing the people in our lives into camps of good and bad. It seemed to make it easier for her to put bad men into "Dad's camp," even though she was the one who had brought them in.

When the man came, my mom was "asleep" on the couch. We were told to leave her alone and let her sleep. I followed the rule, so I wouldn't be punished. But that morning, she had also told me that a man would be bringing something by that I should accept.

Because I had been given conflicting commands, when there was a knock on the door, I answered it.

A young, muscularly built man was standing in our doorway. I thought he looked like one of those surfer dudes you saw on TV. He was younger than my parents. He wore a dirty white T-shirt and reeked of cigarettes.

He asked if Veda was home. I told him she was asleep on the couch.

"Let me see," he said. He leaned through the open doorway, and I pointed to my mom.

"See…there." I was confident that he could tell she was passed out.

He looked angry. "I have these pills that she wants, but she owes me money. I'm not leaving this time without it."

My baby brother, Austin, was not even a year old and was taking a nap, and Tawny was playing alone in the bedroom. I did not want them to see this man.

"How much does she owe you?" I asked.

"A hundred bucks for last week's pills and one hundred for this week."

I was only seven, so I didn't really know how much that was, but I began feeling uncomfortable and that we were not safe. Especially my sister.

He squinted at me. "That's two hundred dollars, little girl, and that's a lot of money."

I had never seen two hundred dollars before, but it sounded like a lot.

I nervously twisted my mouth. "I'll ask Mom to call you when she wakes up."

He leaned in again, looking at my mom on the couch, and smirked. "Seems she won't be waking up for a while."

I knew he was right, and I also feared that Tawny might come looking for me soon, but I just stood there. I wasn't sure of what to do.

"Do you have a bathroom I can use?" he asked.

I pointed down the hall. "It's down there."

He looked at me for a few seconds. "You should come with me."

Even at seven, I knew this wasn't a good idea, but I also knew that if I tried to wake my mom, that might be worse. He might hurt her or all of us. I figured the best thing was for him to just leave as soon as possible, so I followed him down the hall.

I stopped and pointed at the door. "That's the bathroom."

He grabbed my arm, pulled me into the bathroom with him, and locked the door.

"Listen," he said. "You can help your mom out and never see me again. Would you like that?"

I was scared, but I didn't want him to know it. "Yes."

"Good, this won't take long, and if you do what I say, you can have the pills."

What was probably just a few minutes seemed like forever. He pulled down his pants then pushed me down to my knees. The man stunk of more than just the cigarettes. I looked at his penis, which he was now holding in front of me. He told me to open my mouth. I still didn't know what he was going to do, but I did as he said. He shoved himself inside my small mouth. Then he grabbed the back of my head and thrust himself into my throat. I couldn't breathe. My head was throbbing, and tears were streaming down my face.

When he pulled out, I grabbed the toilet and threw up, still reeling with pain.

He just laughed. Then he knelt beside me. "That wasn't so bad, was it?"

I didn't answer. I thought it was.

He grinned and handed me the pills. "Here they are, just like I promised."

It was a painful and humiliating experience that left me feeling dirty and shameful. I will never know this man's name, and I guess that's for the best, but I will never forget his face or his cruel smile. He satisfied his thirst for taking something that did not belong to him, confident that his secret would never be found out. What twisted excuse can a grown man have to violate a small girl, robbing her of her innocence and childhood. After all these years, I still am incapable of understanding that level of depravity.

"Tell your mom that the debt is paid," he said. "And if you promise to never say a word, I won't come back here. Do you understand?"

"Yes."

"Do you promise you won't tell anyone?"

"Yes."

The only relief I could give myself was to tell myself that he never saw me cry. The man never returned, and I never told anyone.

Until now.

CHAPTER FOUR

You Can't Take My Dad

As I wrote earlier, we were never in one place for very long. Every place we lived smelled like smoke. The air was always musty.

Sometimes, we would be somewhere just long enough for me to make a new friend. I have some fond childhood memories of those times. One of my favorites was getting a Fanta Red Cream Soda out of the machine at a motel we were staying at. Other times, we found trouble. Once, I got caught smoking a cigarette in the back of a motel. The truth was, I didn't really like cigarettes. In fact, I threw up the first time I tried one, but smoking made me feel adult and empowered. I think I needed that to feel safe.

No matter where we lived, I never seemed to escape the draft in my bones. Whether we lived in an apartment, hotel, drug rehabilitation center, friend's or family's houses, or foster homes, the walls always felt cold to me. It wasn't until I was an adult that I realized the cold feeling that surrounded me was an inward expression of not feeling safe or welcome.

One night, we were staying in a dodgy little motel on State Street when my mom shouted, "Lynn, they're here!"

I didn't know who she was talking about, but my dad went to the hideaway couch, threw the cushions off, and climbed underneath. I sat on top of the cushions. As I sat there, reveling in being back with my father, there was a loud knock on the door. Mom opened it to police officers.

"What do you want?" she asked.

"We're looking for Lynn Anderson," said one officer.

"He's not here."

The two officers showed their badges and walked inside. "Sorry, we need to look around and see for ourselves," said the officer. "We have a warrant. He's wanted for check fraud."

"Like I said," my mom insisted, "he's not here."

The other policeman shook his head and, with amusement in his voice, said, "Ma'am, I can see him under the cushions." They walked into the room.

I was just eight years old, but I felt like I had to protect my father.

"You can't take my dad!" I screamed.

They did anyway.

Looking back, I feel sorrier for the officer than I do for myself. One officer picked me up while I was kicking and screaming profanities at him, calling him every name I had ever heard my parents call each other, which must have been surprising to him. He gently restrained me while the other officer handcuffed my father. It was horribly painful to see my dad hauled off in handcuffs. That night changed everything for all of us. *Everything*.

CHAPTER FIVE

Losing God

WHEN THEY PUT MY DAD IN JAIL, it triggered a court-ordered drug rehabilitation program for my parents and a state intervention. They labeled Tawny, Austin, and me as "neglected."

Over the next few years, our life became a juggling act of being cared for by friends, family members, and foster care. Now and then, they let us stay with Mom if she had a stable place to live.

To me, foster care felt like waiting, waiting, waiting for the next place to go. I never felt secure because I knew the people with the state could move me at any minute. I was prepared with my large black garbage bag to pack up everything I owned in about ninety seconds. I started taking pride that I could do it so quickly.

I had no control over my life. None. Moves were unannounced and usually unexplained. I never knew when or where I would be going or if I would ever be coming back.

Eventually, I got faster at packing my garbage bag because with each home I stayed at, more of my things would disappear. Nothing was safe, and nothing was mine. I had to borrow everything. The only real constant of my possessions was the garbage bag I moved things in.

It was during this time I asked some very deep existential questions: Who did I belong to? Who, if anyone, cared about me? And how could I be sure of anything in a world of uncertainty?

In foster care, they constantly asked me to adjust to other people's beliefs and religion, which confused me about my own. They told me how to feel and believe, and I was baptized repeatedly into the life description of whatever family I lived with. Pretty soon, I began to question this God that everyone talked about. He didn't feel like *my* God. Maybe he wasn't. Maybe he didn't know about me or my family.

I was never sure when I should express my feelings, risk criticism, or just keep my mouth shut. The questions were pretty much always the same. When I move, will someone write to me or check on me? Will my caseworker come back to see if I am safe? Was I moved because of something I did or did I say something that caused them to send me away? If so, I wanted to know what I'd done or said so I could not do it again. Even though I acted like nothing hurt me, deep down, I really hoped that someone would let me stay.

Even though every family was different, the rules I'd adopted for myself were always the same; don't look too pretty or ugly, don't be too smart or dumb, stay unseen in the shadows. I learned to be helpful but not more than the other kids in the family, or I wouldn't be accepted. I learned how to fight to defend myself. I frequently feared someone might hurt me, emotionally or physically. I was told, many times, by these caretakers that I was lucky to have them, and they didn't owe me anything. I believed them.

I learned to be skeptical long before I knew what the word meant. If someone was nice, they probably wanted something. I learned not to trust nice—I could only trust myself.

Drug rehabilitation centers were not any better than foster care; in fact, everything seemed backward. Adults in rehab would take turns watching each other's kids while their parents got the "help" they needed to be better parents. In other words, unstable people were watching over other unstable people's kids. I was told they were all my mom and dad's friends.

Friends became a misunderstood word. Would friends physically, sexually, or mentally abuse you? I learned the hard way the answer was *yes*. At least with the people my parents would call "friends."

CHAPTER SIX

The Tweaky Man

As my mom went to rehab, my dad was arrested again. This time, Tawny, Austin, and I were all placed in different foster homes. One day, Tawny and I went to visit my mom. During that visit, a man who claimed to be my mother's friend was put in charge of me and my siblings while my mother was in a therapy appointment. I had agreed to help with the laundry while they were away.

The man was about my father's age. He was tall and lanky with oily, spiked hair, and sores on his face and arms. He wore a dirty T-shirt, greasy jeans, and work boots.

After we had left the group, the man put his hand on my shoulder. "Let's go check on the clothes."

Something about the way he said this worried me. Especially since he was "tweaky"—a word I'd learned about how people on drugs moved.

I looked around, but there was no one in sight. Most of all, I was anxious about Tawny. *Where was she?*

"I need to find my sister," I said.

"She's fine," the man said. "She's out in the yard playing with the other kids."

"I better make sure." As I turned to walk away, he grabbed me by the back of my hair and pulled me to him.

"I said she's fine." He spun me around and brought my face close to his. His breath smelled of cigarettes. "There's no one here. Now, come on." He pulled me down the hallway leading to the basement's laundry room. When I started to protest, he covered my mouth with his hand and picked me up around the waist with his other hand. He let go of my mouth for just a second to open the door, step on the landing, and closed the door with his foot.

My mind was reeling; I didn't even think to scream. No one would have heard me anyway unless they were in the laundry room, and no one was there. This was by design as the residents had strict assigned times they could use the facility. Of course, this guy knew that, and more importantly, he knew my mother trusted him.

We got to the bottom of the long staircase, and he opened another door then closed it behind us. A couple of washing machines were running, background noise to cover his dirty work. A single, bare light hung from the ceiling.

Even though I was only eight, I knew what this man wanted from me. As scared as I was, I had no idea how to get out of it. I remember thinking that I'd already been through what he was going to make me do, so I just accepted my fate. I also figured that if I didn't fight, it would be over sooner. I was just grateful that it was me and not Tawny.

The man shoved me over by a washing machine, put quarters in the machine's coin slot then pushed me forward to the floor. I remember the floor was dirty, and there was animal hair on the concrete. The cement was cold, but not as cold as he was. It was as though he had no recognition of me as another human being, let alone a child. I was just there, on all fours, an object to satisfy his lust.

I tried to think of something other than what was happening, but I couldn't. The truth was, I didn't expect this to happen to me in this place. I had expected that I would be safe with the adults who were in the same situation as my parents. I just couldn't fathom what was happening.

The man was standing behind me, and in an instant, his hands were all over me. He unbuttoned my pants then pulled them down, fiercely groping me. I stared at the floor and the walls. The moment turned into the surreal. I noticed the paint on the ceiling was peeling. The light and shadow in the room changed as the lightbulb swung above me.

Like the time I was raped in the bathroom in the apartment, my spirit seemed to slip out of my body. This horror was happening to someone else. I did not feel any pain; I was just numb. The washing machine was spinning. I watched its slight rock. My thoughts began to drift. I wondered where Tawny was. I wondered whose clothes were in the washing machine.

Almost as suddenly as it started, it was over.

"Get up," the man growled. He looked anxious.

I climbed to my feet, pulled my pants up, and buttoned them. All I could think about was what my mom and dad would think if they found out. I was so embarrassed. *They must never know.*

The man walked ahead of me and opened the door. I guessed he expected me to go outside with the other kids. As I started to the door, he said, "Don't say a word about this to anyone."

"I won't," I said. I knew the drill. As I walked outside, he grabbed my arm. "You heard me, right? Because I know where your little sister is."

Anger swept over me like a tsunami. I jerked my arm away from him. "I said I won't! And don't you ever touch my little sister!"

I ran out to Tawny before he could say anything else. She was just innocently playing with the other children. As I leaned against the brick building, for the first time, I felt the physical pain of his violation. My vagina stung, and there was blood running down my legs. It felt like I had been torn. I closed my eyes for a few seconds, trying not to cry.

"Hi, Celeste!" Tawny said when she saw me. "Want to play with us?"

I shook my head. "No, it's almost dinner time."

Tawny was okay, I told myself. *That's all that mattered.*

That night, I found myself thinking of ways to kill that man. I knew I would figure out a way if he ever touched my sister.

CHAPTER SEVEN

Negotiations

NOT LONG AFTER MY RAPE, my mother was sent to a rehab center that allowed children. My mom and Austin went by bus, and Tawny and I, alongside a caseworker, flew to Michigan to meet them.

This center was like a large apartment building with three wings. There was a courtyard in the middle where mothers and children could spend time together on the weekends. Still, I rarely saw my mom. She was in level one of her rehabilitation program and was required to be at level three before she would be allowed to spend extended time with us.

I also rarely saw Austin. He was only about six months old, so the staff took care of him. At least, what staff there was. The center was extremely understaffed, so the children weren't properly supervised. That meant Tawny and I were at the mercy of the hormonal, raging teenage boys and mean adolescent girls. Even at my age, I recognized it was a horrible idea to just throw us all together, unsupervised, regardless of age or gender. *How could they not have thought of that?*

Every day, we rode buses from the center to school. When we returned to the facility, we were supposed to go to our bedroom in our "wing." Then an hour before dinner, they divided us, boys in one place and girls in another, so that we could do our homework. But, in actuality, we just went wherever we wanted to.

The one upside to this environment was that I learned survival skills, including looking for other's weaknesses while never showing my own. In addition, I learned to strike first and to never show fear. Those defensive instincts would stay with me and serve me even into adulthood.

In this place, there were two girls who were the meanest people I had ever encountered, and that's saying something considering my past experiences. Almost daily, they threatened to beat up Tawny. They taunted her constantly, never letting her play in peace. When they got the chance, they would push or trip one of us then walk away. Almost as painful, they made fun of us in front of the other kids. Tawny was an easy target because she was so sweet and kind, and since she didn't defend herself, they bullied her the most. In the center's bizarre *Lord of the Flies* culture, there was an unspoken cool tribe. Tawny and I were not part of it.

One day after school, I followed those two girls to their room to confront them. My anger made me feel powerful, even though I had no idea what I would say. As I approached them, one girl said, "Coming to take one for the team?" They both laughed.

I had no idea what that meant, but I knew we would not just talk.

"You're just a loser," the other said. "You and your stupid sister. Your parents don't even want you."

Anger welled inside me. I suddenly felt like a crazy person. That's when I burst.

Looking around for whatever weapon I could find, I grabbed two naked barbie dolls from the floor and then charged at the teenager who had been talking. I was swinging wildly, slamming the dolls as hard as I could into her face. Blood splattered around us. Though her face was covered with blood, all I could see was the sadistic smirk she always had on her face as she and her friends bullied my sister and me. I was out of my mind, and my only goal was to inflict as much pain as possible. I didn't care if I killed her. The fury that had been building inside me was out of control—every hurt I had experienced in this horrible place, every second I tried to protect my sister, never feeling safe, was unleashed on this girl nearly twice my age. I hit and hit her until her face was a bloody mess.

The second girl tried to get me off her but couldn't. I have no idea how long the fight lasted before two staff members pulled me off her. They locked me in a padded room to cool off.

I had beat the girl's face so severely she was hospitalized. I didn't care at all. I only cared that they didn't hurt my little sister and me anymore. I was beginning to learn how to navigate this world. If this was going to be my life, I needed to learn to be mean like the rest of them. Not just mean but clever. That's what it took to survive.

One night, a group of us sneaked into an empty conference room with a VCR. One kid had gotten a copy of a movie called *The Exorcist*. I was glad to be invited to watch since it meant I was now accepted by the cool tribe after beating that girl so badly. I figured that Tawny and I were safe. Again, I was wrong.

After school the next week, I noticed three boys, about fourteen or fifteen years old, talking to Tawny. One of them smiled and played with her hair. I had just turned eight, and Tawny was about to turn six.

I recognized that look and knew they wanted something more from Tawny. I decided to offer them a deal. After all, if I could give the creepy man with the dirty T-shirt something not to come back, why couldn't I do it with these guys? I couldn't imagine anything worse; I survived the horrible man in the laundry room and didn't die. I just wanted to protect Tawny.

That night at the "cool kids tribe," I walked up to the boy who had been playing with Tawny's hair. "Hey," I said.

The boy looked surprised that I had approached him. "What?" he grunted.

"I want to make a deal with you."

"For what?"

"For you to keep away from my sister."

His eyes narrowed. He glanced furtively at his two friends then looked back at me. "What do you have in mind?"

I folded my arms and looked directly into his eyes. "Talk to your friends and let me know what you want."

He grinned. "Really?"

"Yeah," I said.

He nodded. "Okay."

I thought I was so tough to negotiate with these older boys. I had no idea what I was in for, but it was one way of being in control in a world where I had so little control. Or none.

The next morning, the boy approached me. "I talked to my friends," he said. "There's a room in the basement at the bottom of the stairs. Meet us there at midnight, and we'll show you what we want."

I just nodded and walked away. I didn't have a watch, or even a clock, so I really didn't know when midnight was. I did know the one time my mom was allowed to see me was at 11:00 p.m. when she would say goodnight and lay out my clothes on my bed.

That night after she left my room, I waited until everything was quiet then headed down the hallway. I wore nothing but my nightgown, and the hall tile was cold on my bare feet. I went slowly down the three flights of stairs in the dark. I wasn't scared, but I was nervous.

I had never been to this part of the building. The large unfinished basement was dingy, dusty, and full of cobwebs.

I remember thinking it would be a great place to play hide-and-seek.

The boys were waiting for me at the bottom of the stairs. The boy I had made the offer to said they had talked about what they wanted from me, so they would leave my sister alone.

I tried to look tough and older than I was. "Okay, what?"

One boy seemed to be in charge, but he was a different boy than the one I had made the offer to. He put his hand on my shoulder. "We want you to let us do whatever we want to you. No questions, no yelling, no fighting back."

I didn't hesitate. I pushed his hand off my shoulder. "When?"

"Right now," he said.

It seemed they had planned things. One boy took my hand, and I followed him into a mechanical room where there was a loud furnace, a bunch of old desks, and furniture that had been broken and abandoned—a perfect spot for their plan.

There was an old stained mattress on the floor. I wasn't sure if it was already there or if the boys had dragged it from someplace else. I noticed they had brought some things—sheets, Vaseline, and a bandanna, probably for a gag, I thought. They didn't need it. I wasn't going to scream.

The kid in charge said, "Take your nightgown off and lay down on the bed."

I obeyed. I pulled the gown off over my head, standing nude in front of the boys. For a moment, they just stared.

Then I dropped my gown to the floor and lay back on the bed. I felt oddly brave that I was doing something for my little sister that our mom had never done for me. I aimed to protect Tawny, so she didn't have to go through what I had. As far as I knew, I had succeeded. For the first time, I felt much older than I really was. Somehow, lying on my back, at the mercy of three teenage boys, I felt strong.

Two of the boys were skinny. The third was heavier, short, and seemed more nervous than the others as if he really didn't want to be there. I wondered if it was his first time doing something like this. The other two seemed to know exactly what they wanted to do to me.

One at a time, they did what they wanted to do with me. At first, the heavier boy just looked at me sadly, but the other two ridiculed him until he went along. For more than an hour, this went on, like a lewd tag team event. When one boy finished, another would take over. They did everything they could imagine. I wondered if they had seen pictures of these acts in a magazine or watched a dirty movie to learn how to do what they were doing. Again, in my mind, I was transported to another place.

The room was dark, except for the flame in the furnace. I remember just watching the flame as I had the washing machine the last time I was raped. Colors of purple, yellow, and orange danced around. As I stared into the flame, my mind went to the baseball field, where my dad and I would sing, "Take Me Out to the Ballgame," and eat peanuts. I didn't cry. Never Celeste, never cry. No tears. No tears.

To this day, when I see a flame in a fire, it sparks the memories of that night. That's when, in my young mind, I won Tawny's safety. No matter what it did to me, I wasn't a victim. Finally, I was the victor.

CHAPTER EIGHT

A Room Full of Men

I HAD BELIEVED THE "DEAL" I had made with those boys would finally bring Tawny and me peace. But within a few days of that night in the basement, my mother came into my room to talk to me. I was certain she had somehow found out about the boys, and that I was in trouble for what I had done.

Instead, Mom told me that Tawny and Austin were being sent back to Salt Lake City, and that she and I were going to another drug rehabilitation center in New York. She said we were going there so that the two of us would have time to work out the problems in our relationship.

I was angry. My mother and I had *never* got along, and now Tawny and Austin were being taken from me again. Mom and I had never stopped fighting over who was in charge—who really was the mother. She was certain she was the mother, and legally, she was right even if she didn't act like it. She was simply incapable of making grown-up decisions. It was as if *protecting* or caring for her children had never even crossed her mind. I clearly did a better job of it. I could never understand why she didn't see it. Or maybe she did. Maybe that's why she hated me so much. For as long as I could remember, I had been making maternal decisions regarding my little brother and sister, while everyone else made decisions *for* my mom—the counselors, the courts, sometimes even me.

During our interview with the counselors, it was determined that due to my "behavioral issues," I would need to be in a program with my mom that provided more supervision and a more extensive therapy program. I was actually told that "I was a danger to my brother and sister."

I don't have the words to describe the fury I felt hearing this. For all those years, it was me who protected them—who did what was necessary to make sure they were taken care of. Now, I was being accused of being a danger to them, and that I was the reason we were split up again. Even now, it's still difficult for me to get my head around this evaluation by so-called professionals.

Didn't they know how hard I tried? Didn't they know what I had gone through to protect my little sister? I began to truly feel hatred toward everyone around me, especially my mom. I was still a little kid. Where was *she in all of this*? I would never forgive her for that.

Soon after arriving in New York, I began having night terrors from the abuse I had been through. When I would drift off to sleep, I would wake up screaming from a dream about men, boys, darkness, or pain. Sometimes, I couldn't tell what was real and what wasn't.

For several days in a row, they took me to a room with a therapist and given sleeping pills. I would lie on a table until I fell asleep. I'd wake the next morning in my bed. Whatever they had given me worked because I could sleep. In fact, I would sleep so soundly that I couldn't remember dreaming, which I was grateful for. I never had good dreams.

When I talked to my biological mom about this book, she said that when they took me to a room to talk to me, they always closed the door, and she never knew what was going on inside. She said it made her uncomfortable that no one ever explained, but she just went along with whatever she was told. She figured the professionals always knew what was best for all of us.

Around this time, I started meeting with a wonderful therapist named Candace who my mother said was my godmother. She was the first black woman I had met in the system—a strong-willed woman whose very presence demanded respect just by walking into a room. I admired her strength so much. She never took crap from anyone, including me, and she always spoke her mind without hesitation.

I had never been around this type of fiercely powerful woman, and we became very close. She started taking me places so that I could experience healthy activities outside the shelter or rehab environment. She took me out to ice cream or to fun places like Coney Island. I think she wanted me to feel like a child again. It was empowering to talk to someone that really listened and seemed to understand me.

For the first time in my life, someone was paying attention to me, and it felt good. I missed Tawny and Austin, but I was starting to feel better about myself. Things were beginning to change for the better, and I realized that possibly someone could help me and my mom have a better relationship. Then maybe, eventually, we could all be together as a family again. At least I hoped.

I had been working with Candace for about two months when a woman I'd never seen before came into my room and asked me to follow her. All I was told was that I needed to answer some questions.

My first thought was, *What had I done wrong?* I racked my brain. I hadn't been fighting with anyone or had any bad behavior experiences with men. I was so confused and scared.

Without speaking, I followed the woman down the long tile corridor, our footsteps echoing behind us. No matter what facility I was in, it seemed like I was always following someone down a hallway.

We stopped at a door that was partially open. I peered

around the woman and into the room. I could see my mom sitting at the end of a couch. There were a whole lot of men, some sitting, some standing. After we walked in, I realized that there were even more men. Nothing about this felt good. Considering the audience, I was sure I was in serious trouble.

The woman closed the door behind us. I looked around at all the people then pushed myself back against the wall. *Why were all these men looking at me?*

I looked at my mom for an explanation, but as usual, she just looked away—once again abandoning me in my time of need. This was common for her when there was something she couldn't handle. She was like a turtle that way, pulling her head in at the first sign of trouble.

My experience with strange men was that they told me to take my clothes off. *Is that what they were going to do?* I was preparing mentally to do whatever it took to make it all go away, *even* if my mom was in the room. She probably wouldn't care, anyway.

I looked at her again. This time my eyes rested on her hoping she would say something. Anything. She didn't. But she did cry, which was something.

One of the men said, "Can you tell us what happened in Salt Lake City."

I looked at him for a moment then said, "I don't know what you're talking about." I really didn't. So much had happened in Salt Lake City that I wasn't sure which story I was supposed to tell.

Another man said, "Celeste, we know that something happened with one of your mother's friends in the drug rehabilitation center you were visiting."

My face turned hot. *How did they find out?*

The man continued. "It's okay to tell us. You're not in any trouble. We just need to hear it from you."

If I wasn't in trouble, then why was I in a room with so many men staring at me.

Now I knew they were talking about the man who had raped me in the basement of the rehab center next to the washers and dryers. In spite of his assurance otherwise, I knew I was in trouble.

I shook my head. "Nothing," I said. I wasn't talking. There was no way I was going to tell strangers about something so humiliating and could possibly endanger my sister. I was taking this to my grave. "I'm not going to tell you anything about that."

My mom cried even more, and I glanced at her again. Again, she was no help.

Then another man said, "You don't have to tell us, Celeste. We know what happened. He already admitted it. In fact, he bragged about it, and now he's in jail."

Then why in the hell am I in here being humiliated if he's already in jail? I thought. All I said was, "Can I go now?"

"Yes," said one of the men.

I didn't know which man it was because I was looking at my mom waiting for something. She just looked at the floor and cried.

I turned and walked out of the room. I couldn't believe what had just happened. Even as a little girl, I knew it made no sense to take a child into a room of strangers and further traumatize her by asking her to talk about something that painful.

Later that day, Candace came into my room. "I'm so sorry about how that was handled. They were hoping that your story could convince the judge to extend that man's jail time."

"I just thought that was all over with," I mumbled angrily.

"I know. I'm sorry." Candace didn't say anymore. She just gave me a hug then left me alone.

Again, when I talked to my mom while writing this book, I asked her if she knew the man's name who had hurt me—the one who went to jail.

"No," she said. "He was just one of your 'dad's friends.'"

CHAPTER NINE

The Final Blow

*S*TILL IN NEW YORK about two weeks after what felt like an interrogation with all those men, my mom asked if she could talk to me alone. We never talked alone, so I thought she was going to tell me she was sorry for what had happened in that room and for not protecting me.

Instead, she started crying. Suddenly, the room felt like it was closing in on me. Smothering me. I knew she was going to say something horrible. She didn't disappoint.

"We didn't come to New York to work on our problems," she blurted.

I looked at her quizzically. "Then why did we come here?"

"Because Tawny and Austin were sent to Salt Lake City to be adopted." She paused. "Now you're going to Salt Lake City to be adopted, too."

Suddenly, the mood changed. I assumed that meant I would be adopted along with Tawny and Austin. "I get to be with them?"

Mom looked back down. "No, they're being adopted into a different family than you. That family can't take three children."

I had been lied to, *again*. At that moment, everything felt like slow motion. For a few seconds, I couldn't breathe at all. Though my body was frozen, my mind was reeling with a hundred different questions.

Tawny and Austin were being taken from me, *again*. How was I supposed to save our family now? For the first time that I remember, I cried in front of my mom.

"Please," I sobbed. "Don't let them do this. I'll be a better daughter, I promise. I'm sorry I've been so much trouble…" I fell on the floor crying uncontrollably, clinging to hope that what she'd told me wasn't true.

My mom knelt on the floor next to me, and we cried. We cried and cried until there were no more tears. Then we cried some more. This is the one and only time in my life I recall us crying together.

Tragically, the decision had already been set in motion. There was nothing I could do. I couldn't talk or manipulate my way out of this one.

"Your parents weren't given a choice, Celeste," Candace explained. "The state decided that they needed too much help, and taking care of three children has proven to be impossible for them."

I sat quietly trying to understand.

"You're going to fly to Salt Lake City. Your dad will meet you at the airport with the caseworker."

The sadness I felt was so heavy. The only bright side was that I was going to see my dad. I hadn't seen him for over a year.

The next day, a caseworker drove us to the airport. My mom was silent the whole way. Back then, people could accompany passengers right to the gate, and a parent could actually take their child onto the plane. My mom held my hand and walked me down the long jet bridge and to my seat. Because I was a child traveling alone, I had a window seat in the first row with no one in front of me. A stewardess welcomed us but stood a way off while my mom said goodbye. She could tell this was emotional for the both of us.

This was the first time I remembered my mother taking charge of situation, and I felt like I really had a mom. She put my garbage sack in the overhead bin then buckled my seatbelt. She held my hands and looked into my eyes with tears streaming down her cheeks. I think we both felt we had failed. There was nothing left to say. Then she hugged me and kissed my forehead.

"I love you, Celeste."

I was flooded with mixed emotions of anger, sadness, regret, and loneliness.

Mom hugged me one more time, and then she turned and walked off the plane. I watched her until I couldn't see her anymore. I wondered if I would ever see her again. I felt numb.

I stared out the window the entire flight to Salt Lake City. I had no idea what was happening next. Most of all, I was confused. I had been so certain that things were getting better for us and believed we would all be back together soon. I had not processed anything different. It was incomprehensible to me that I'd never see Tawny or Austin again.

In my world, I believed there was no way they could keep us apart. Why would they separate us? Why would we be in different families? Maybe someone would see that they'd made a mistake and fix this. I couldn't understand, and I didn't want to. Tawny and Austin were all I had left in the world, and now I had nothing. They were taking it all away. They were taking my life away.

CHAPTER TEN

Funyuns and Chocolate Milk

WHEN THE PLANE LANDED in Salt Lake City, my father wasn't there. More lies.

"Where's my dad?" I asked angrily. "They said he would be here."

The caseworker had a kind face. "He couldn't come today, but he's picking you up bright and early Saturday, and the two of you will spend the entire day together."

I stared out the car window on the drive to the temporary foster home, where I was being kept until my adoption, wondering if this was another lie. When we arrived at the foster home, I begged one of my new foster sisters to let me borrow an outfit. I had nothing to give her in return except a week of chores, so I promised that. I was so excited to see my dad. I tried to bury the pain in my heart since this would be my last day with him. I wanted this day to be perfect.

The next morning couldn't have come fast enough, and I could barely sleep the night before. He was coming at 7:00 a.m. We had a whole house of foster children, so I showered that night, so I wouldn't wake anyone up. Things were always better if I remained invisible.

I was awake by 5:00 a.m. I quietly got both mine and my foster sister's chores done. My foster mom had told me I could not go with my dad unless I did my chores, and I believed her. I'm not sure why anyone would have made that kind of threat—to deprive a girl of seeing her father for the last time ever because of some inconsequential chores—but at that point, I would have agreed to anything.

I got myself dressed and then slid my mattress under the bed, leaving no sign that I had ever been there or even existed. I folded my bedding and clothes neatly in a corner and placed them next to my garbage bag full of my things. Then I waited on the front porch until a van pulled in the driveway.

My caseworker was driving, but I could see that my dad was in the passenger seat. It wasn't a lie! He looked just as I had remembered. They both got out of the van and walked toward me.

"Dad!" Crying, I ran right past my caseworker and jumped into my dad's arms, giving him the longest hug. I hugged and hugged him. They had told me this was our last visit together, and I would not be allowed to see him until I was eighteen, should he agree to see me.

"What should we do today?" he asked.

"I don't care," I said happily. "We can do anything as long as we're together."

I truly meant that. When my dad was sober, he was my happy place. He always told me how proud he was of me, how smart I was, and that I would grow up to do great things. He was the only one ever to tell me that. I was never sure if I believed any of it, considering how screwed up our life was, but every child wants to hear those things from a parent. So, when he said he was proud of me, I held that close to my heart.

I turned back and asked the caseworker, "Do we get to see Tawny and Austin, too?"

She shook her head. "I'm sorry. Their adoption is already in place."

"What about my grandma, grandpa, uncles, aunts, and cousins? Can I at least say goodbye to everyone?"

"No, Celeste, I'm sorry," the caseworker said again.

I realized that my entire life as I knew it was ending. That after today, everything that had brought me joy would be gone, and I could do nothing about it. My heart sank for the zillionth time in my eight short years. It was just one more reminder that anything I wanted was unimportant. That I was unimportant. I took a deep breath, forced back the tears, and returned my focus to my dad.

He took my hand. "Let's get this day started. I have lots planned for us."

In bureaucratic legalese, this would be an "unsupervised" visit, so the caseworker gave us a few rules, then we were off.

Our first stop was the drug rehab where my dad was currently living. He brought out a large box of small, wrapped gifts—one for Easter, Valentine's, Christmas, and my birthday. He watched me open each one. He had planned to celebrate as many holidays as possible, knowing they would be our last. I could tell he had spent a lot of time planning this out.

My favorite gift was a *Black Beauty* book for my birthday that Dad had signed. He knew I loved horses. It was also important to my dad that we did my favorite things, so we went to a baseball game in the afternoon and played board games until dinner. Later that evening, we walked to a movie theater, and while I cannot remember what movie we saw, I will never forget our walk home.

Dad insisted on carrying me. Even with his limp, he still did it. A person would usually carry an eight-year-old on piggyback, but Dad held me like an infant, with my head cradled in one arm and my legs dangling over his other. He looked into my eyes when he talked to me. I knew this had to be hard for him physically—I was a big girl, not a tiny baby—and he was always in pain.

"Do you know what polio is, Celeste?"

I shook my head. "No."

"It's a disease that affects the spinal cord, causing muscle weakness and pain. Sometimes, even our bones get smaller."

I was trying to picture how that would happen because as I grew, my bones grew bigger. "Is that why you always hurt?"

He nodded. "When I was born, there weren't any shots

to prevent it, so they gave me medicine for pain when I was a baby. I was addicted to the medicine by the time I was fifteen."

"Will I get it?"

He hugged me reassuringly then said, "You don't need to worry. You've had a polio shot. You'll never get it."

I nodded, hoping it wasn't a lie to make me feel good.

"Do you know what *addiction* means?"

I had heard the word before, but I shook my head.

"It's when your body needs something, and if it doesn't get it, you feel pain." He frowned. "The thing is, Celeste, when a person is addicted to something, they will do anything to get what their body needs, even if it means putting their family in harm's way." His eyes filled with tears. "That's what happened to me."

"Do you love your medicine more than me?" I asked.

"No, sweetie. I will never love anything as much as I love you. I've tried many times to quit, and it hasn't worked."

"Can you try something else?"

Now tears spilled freely down his cheeks as he spoke. "I wish it were that simple," he said. "That's why I'm in this drug rehab. I'm still trying, but the state says I have had enough chances."

I cried, too. "I'll wait for you to get better, Daddy."

"I know you will, baby. But they won't let me see you again after today."

Even though I believed him, my young mind could not grasp the reality or totality of it. I didn't mean to make it so hard for my dad that night, but I couldn't stop crying. I couldn't imagine my life without him, my brother and sister, and the rest of our extended family.

He pulled me closer. "What I want to tell you is important, so I need you to listen and promise me you'll tell your brother and sister too someday. Can you do that?"

Though I couldn't stop crying, I nodded. "Okay, Daddy," I said even though I wondered if I would ever get the chance to tell Tawny and Austin anything at all.

He started to talk again, but his voice caught with emotion. He stopped for a few seconds. Finally, he said, "What has happened to you, and what will happen next, is not your fault. It has never been your fault. You have been a great daughter and big sister, and your mom and I love you very much. So, always remember you did nothing wrong and do not deserve what has happened." He stopped, crying too hard to continue until he caught his breath. "I'm so, so sorry, sweetie."

His crying made me cry even more. "It's okay, Daddy," I said again. "I'll tell them, I promise. We'll be okay."

But I lied. I knew we were not going to be okay. None of us would. We both cried without talking anymore the rest of the way back. There were no more words to say.

It was late by the time we got back to the van. My dad put me down, wiped the tears from his cheeks, and grinned. "I have one more surprise for you on our way back."

I could not imagine what it might be. The best surprise would be that we were all going back home, wherever that was. We loaded all my gifts into a box and put them in the van. I tried to be excited, but my stomach hurt too much. I had felt this agony before but never this extreme. The feeling was horrible—an awful combination of disappointment, loneliness, sadness, and fear of the unknown.

As my dad pulled into a 7-11 parking lot, I knew exactly what we were doing. I looked at him and smiled. "I know what this is."

He smiled back. I jumped out of the van then ran around to my dad. He took my hand. We went inside, made our purchase, and returned to the van. It was my father's and my special thing—Funyuns and chocolate milk.

Today, I'm not sure what was so wonderful about those two things, but when I was a little girl with my dad, it was our favorite treat, right up there with peanuts at the ballgame. On the way back to the foster home, we ate in silence.

Then it was time to say goodbye. My dad was emotional. I promised myself not to cry anymore, so I wouldn't make it harder for him. Dad walked me to the door, picked me up, and hugged me so tight I thought he would squish me. I didn't care if he did.

I just kept thinking, *No tears. No tears. No tears.*

When he sat me back down, I gave him another quick hug, then I turned and walked inside the house. I set my box down and stood in the doorway while he returned to the van. He started the engine, rolled the window down, and leaned toward me. I could still see the agony on his tear-streaked face. I think he wanted to say something, but he couldn't. There was too much to say.

I called to him, "See you at the baseball game, Dad!"

Inspite of his pain, he smiled, wiped his eyes, then slowly drove away. I looked down at my box with the empty Funyuns wrapper and chocolate milk container on top of my gifts. My little girl's heart sank, and I knew it would be the last time I would share that special snack with my dad.

I closed the door, literally, on my life. I thought of all the times I had protected my sister, and for what? Anything could happen to her now. Would I ever see Tawny and Austin again? Were they together? And what about me? I had nobody. I belonged to nobody. I stood silently, staring at the door. What now?

And I cried.

PART 2

CHAPTER ELEVEN

Who's Buffy?

WHEN I WAS A FOSTER KID, all I had for a suitcase was a big black trash bag—the same kind you put leaves in. They were strong, big enough to hold everything I owned, and easy to pack fast; another thing a foster kid gets good at. In spite of all my losses, I was peculiarly optimistic. I had everything I needed, including the treasures my dad had given me. Most of all, I was going to a home that wanted to adopt me.

My caseworker drove me to meet the Hatts. We arrived at their farm and the biggest house I had ever seen. I was told that my soon-to-be new sister's name was Dana, and she had a massive bedroom with two beds filled with so many toys that she hadn't even opened some of the boxes they came in. *How exciting*, I thought. I was practically moving into a toy store! Maybe the state knew what they were doing. Maybe this might not be so bad after all.

But I soon realized that Dana thought of me as just another unwelcomed toy. When I walked into the house, she looked at me with a confused look on her face. Then she had a complete meltdown.

"She's not Buffy! I chose Buffy. I want Buffy!"

Who the hell was Buffy? I later learned that Dana had picked a girl named Buffy out of a huge binder full of pictures and descriptions of foster kids that were available for adoption. I was not fond of the idea she had chosen me from a binder, like an object in a catalog. Especially now that I knew I wasn't her first choice.

Dana's mom, Kathy, had promised her Buffy for Christmas. But by the time the family had decided to adopt her, she was already gone, leaving me next in line to fill their need. *Well, being second best was better than not being chosen at all*, I thought. I was wrong.

My new mother, Kathy Hatt, tried unsuccessfully to appease Dana.

"I told you that Buffy was adopted. This one will have to do. Please be happy. She's your Christmas present. You don't want to ruin Christmas, do you?"

Dana wasn't having it. She carried on most of that day and begrudgingly showed me her room, continually reminding me I could not touch anything without her permission.

That was my first visit, and I remember leaving with my caseworker that day, thinking how lucky Buffy was not to be adopted by this family. Hopefully, she had been adopted by a loving, caring family who wanted her and wasn't just picked as a toy for their nasty, spoiled daughter.

When I got back to my foster home that day, my foster mother said, "You know, Celeste, you really should be happy. You're so lucky to be adopted. Most older kids don't get adopted and spend their life in foster care. If this family wants you back, you should go."

It was obvious she hadn't met Kathy or Dana—the girl who would soon be my "sister" if you could call her that. I felt more like property than family.

A week later, I was told that I would be staying with the Hatts for a while and to bring all of my belongings. That request still amuses me. All of my *belongings*?

I returned the outfit I had borrowed from my foster sister, rolled up my mattress, then packed my few treasures in my trash bag. I tried to feel lucky like everyone told me I was. Even though it was apparent that Dana was a brat, I thought that once she got to know me, she would like me, and at least I would have a place to sleep. At least that's what I thought. I had been through a lot worse.

I tried to convince myself that being a Christmas gift was okay, however unwanted, and I would be a great big sister to Dana, just like I had been to Tawny. I thought I had been pretty good at that, so this might turn out okay.

Being a Christmas present was even worse than I thought. Dana and the rest of this bizarre family's mindset was that Dana owned me. Literally. And, as her property, there were rules. I could only have the same friends as

Dana. I had to go where she wanted to and leave when she was ready. This meant I had to convince Dana that her friends liked her in hopes that she wouldn't abandon them, and I could have them as friends, too, which took some skill. We were at a neighbor's birthday party when this became a reality for me.

"I want to go now," Dana said abruptly.

I looked over at Dana. "Why? We just started playing games."

"I don't care. We're going home. Mom said when I want to go, we have to leave."

I was following her out of the house when one girl said, "Celeste can stay, Dana."

Dana spun around angrily. "No, she can't. She's mine, and I'm in charge. She goes where I go."

The girl looked rightfully confused. When we got outside and waited for Kathy to pick us up, Dana said, "They don't like me, anyway."

"Yes, they do," I said, trying to sound believable. The truth was, Dana was very unlikeable. I had just met these girls, but it seemed like Dana needed some validation that they did like her, or I would never be able to have play dates with them again. And anything was better than being left in the house with Kathy who loved to remind me I was not her real daughter, and I was lucky to have a family that would take me.

She really did think that way. She made herself seem magnanimous and compassionate when she really was anything but. I was never sure how to please Kathy, or if it was even possible. She would often play cruel psychological mind games with me.

"Celeste!"

I hurried to where she was. She was folding laundry.

"You need to fold your own laundry."

I folded my clothes while she folded the rest of the family's. Travis was my older foster brother, Dana was a year younger than me, and my foster brother, Scott, was the same age. None of the other kids had to fold their laundry—just me. I had always done this before in other homes, but I still thought it was unfair and could not understand why I was singled out.

Another one of her tricks was at bedtime, Kathy would insist that I kiss her on the cheek. But every time I tried, she would quickly turn away so that I would miss her face with my kiss. Bizarrely, it was the same thing night after night. But if I didn't play her game, she would get mad and tell me I was ungrateful.

One morning, I said, "Kathy, I was wondering…"

"What? I'm not good enough for you to call me Mom?"

"No, I just… I'm sorry, Mom."

Kathy twisted her mouth and shook her head. "You do know, of course, I'm not REALLY your mother."

Her games went on and on. I never knew how to be around her or how to make her like me, as hard as I tried.

In my elementary school, we had a music program, and I had the opportunity to play several instruments. I soon realized that, like my father, I had been born with an aptitude for music. It made me happy to still have that connection to my dad. When I was given the chance to play the accordion, I jumped at the opportunity. I practiced every day at home.

One day while I was practicing, Kathy walked up behind me and, wielding a pair of scissors, cut off each of my ponytails. She was all about control, and I knew it, so when the tears came, I didn't even look up. I just kept playing.

"Oops, looks like you'll need a haircut," Kathy said then walked away.

I did have to get a haircut, which looked awful. But that wasn't the worst part. It was Kathy's sadism and control of me. Now, whenever I looked in a mirror, I was reminded of how she both owned and hated me.

Kathy was careful never to verbally abuse me when Kent, her husband, was around because she knew it would anger him. Unfortunately, he was rarely around, and Kathy was a stay-at-home mom. It seemed I could never escape her wrath. One time, I sprained my arm, and the doctor wrapped it. Occasionally, she would walk up to me, grab my arm, and shake it. "Does that still hurt?"

Of course it hurt, and I knew she knew it did, but I would never let her know.

Everything between Kathy and me was about control. I worked hard at not letting her think she had anything over me. I'm sure that made her hate me even more.

On top of that, it was obvious to me, even at the age

of nine, that Kathy and Kent's marriage was falling apart. I later learned that bringing another child into the picture was their last-ditch effort to salvage their deteriorating marriage. But I had just made it worse.

I loved working out on the farm with Kent. I longed for a father/daughter relationship after losing my father. Kent built things and grew things, and I loved learning from him. He taught me to feed the animals, grow vegetables, and, even as small as I was, how to cut and throw hay bales into the back of a truck. I also learned how to irrigate lawns, build dams in ditches, and put up trusses for roofs.

I followed Kent everywhere and learned more and more every day. We built fences, poured concrete, weeded flowers, and mowed lawns. He didn't talk much, he was taciturn by nature, but I always had the feeling that he liked me because I was eager to learn from him and never complained or whined like the other kids.

None of my siblings were interested in working with Kent, and it was obvious to me Kathy hated that he and I grew closer while they continued to drift further apart. While I could see it, I wasn't sure if their three biological kids did. I doubted it. They never really seemed to look beyond themselves.

Staying away from Kathy and Travis, the oldest, was the key to my survival, so spending time with Kent felt like a real solution.

I could never fully understand why Kathy wouldn't love me and why Travis could never like me. I was a good kid, never caused trouble, never talked back, and kept up on my homework. I tried not to overshadow the other kids with too high of grades but to stay even with the rest of my siblings. I did my chores when asked and often did the chores of the other kids, so they would like me, too. I had to be careful, though. If Kathy caught me, she would accuse me of trying to get more of Kent's attention, and that was an entirely different set of issues to deal with.

Years later, I watched a movie called *Ever After* with Drew Barrymore. Drew's character asked her stepmother, "Did you ever love me?"

The stepmother replied, "How could I ever love a pebble in my shoe?"

That's when I realized what I was to Kathy—*a pebble in her shoe.*

CHAPTER TWELVE

False Hope

*C*ASEWORKERS ALWAYS TOLD ME they would come back and check on me, but no one ever did. So, I could tell no one about the abuse that was happening in the home with Kathy.

As my adoption day neared, I realized how much I missed my old family life, dysfunctional as it was, and I would go back there in a heartbeat instead of living with the Hatts. Even though my parents moved us all over the place and horrible things happened to me, I still had Tawny and Austin. I also knew that my parents, unsuccessful as they were, were still trying to hold it together for us. My dad told me he loved me and so did Tawny.

I also had cousins, uncles, and aunts who would let me stay with them from time to time. I even believed that deep down, in her own messed up way, my biological mother loved me, too—something I would *never* have accused Kathy or any of the Hatts of.

In the Hatt world, it was always me vs. them. They frequently reminded me of how unloved and unwanted I was. Truthfully, their constant psychological abuse was worse than any other physical or sexual abuse I had been through.

On the drive to the adoption court, Travis, Dana, Scott, and I rode in the back of their green Ford pickup truck.

"If they ask me if I want you to stay with us," Travis said, "I will say no."

Dana added. "Me, too. This won't make you our real sister, anyway."

I looked over at Scott. He was never as vocal as his brother and sister, but he also nodded. "Me, too."

Sometimes, I think he just played along to avoid the wrath of Travis and Kathy, but regardless, it was unanimous. Even though I said nothing, in reality, I hoped that really would happen. Then I could live somewhere else. *Anywhere else.* At this point, I couldn't imagine that anywhere else could be worse.

As we drove into town, it was my first time seeing something as large and majestic as the City and County Building in downtown Salt Lake City. The massive Richardsonian Romanesque structure built in 1894 was a city landmark that tourists sometimes confused for the Mormon temple.

On the front of the building, the large clock tower was adorned with a Statue of Columbia, an answer to the

Mormon temple's angel Moroni. The building left me with a sense of awe. I thought special things could happen in this building. Maybe even for me.

When we entered the building's spacious marble-floored lobby, I was surprised to see my caseworker there. I had pretty much forgotten about her since I hadn't seen her since she dropped me off at the Hatt's a thousand years ago. I had often hoped she would come back and check on me so that I could tell her all the awful things that were happening to me. But she never did. Not once.

She walked up to me with a smile on her face. "Celeste, I have a wonderful surprise for you."

I couldn't imagine what surprise she could possibly have that would be wonderful. A new family, perhaps?

"Your brother and sister are here, and we arranged it so that you'll all be adopted together. Isn't that wonderful?"

I was ecstatic. Tawny and Austin's caseworkers had told them the same thing, and we all thought this was a reunion to bring us back together. This was a wonderful surprise. All I wanted had finally happened! The powers that be had changed their minds and decided I was good for my siblings, and I wouldn't hurt them after all. I didn't care whose house we would end up in or even what family, just that we would all be together.

Tawny and Austin walked around a corner from a hallway dressed in their Sunday best. It had been a year since I had seen them, but it seemed like forever. I thought they looked so beautiful. We were all crying and hugging, united again and thinking we would finally be together. But we were wrong.

When my caseworker realized what was happening, she stepped in to explain.

"Oh, my goodness, I'm so sorry. Being adopted today means you are all being adopted simultaneously, not into the *same* family."

For a moment, all three of us were in shock. Then we burst into tears. We were living past nightmares all over again. The surprise our caseworkers thought would be special for us was the worst news ever. They reunited us after a year only to finalize our permanent separation all at the same time. It felt like a sadistic joke. I thought I knew what pain was, but this was now the worst ever. The overwhelming feelings of sadness and despair I felt at that moment were something I had never experienced before. I would never see my brother and sister again. That was a hurt I still cannot describe.

My caseworker looked almost ill. She knew she had made a terrible mistake. Being unintentionally cruel is still cruel. Neither of us said a word. I said goodbye to Tawny and Austin (their new family had changed his name to Tommy because all their other children's names started with T) then followed my caseworker into the judge's chamber. A tsunami of sadness overwhelmed me, and I thought that, it didn't matter if I just stayed with the Hatts after all.

I stood before the judge's desk with the Hatt family sitting on couches behind me. They were all looking at the floor, except Kent. He seemed to be the only one who thought this was a good idea. I thought about what the three kids had said to me in the truck, still hoping that moment would come when they would all confess their true feelings of disgust for me, but it didn't happen. Instead, again I was reminded, this time by the judge, that I was lucky to be adopted by the Hatts because "older" children usually do not get this opportunity.

I hated that everyone kept reminding me of that. I was fully aware that I was old, unlovable, and unwanted without them reminding me how *lucky* I was. Was I *lucky* to have lost the only family who would ever love me? Was I *lucky* to be reminded every day that a woman who is supposed to love and care for me hated and neglected me? Was I lucky to never see my brother and sister again and cursed to wonder in ignorance if they were safe or not?

In my mind, I was anything but lucky. I never should have been born into a world that hated me so much. The judge's voice pulled me out of my thoughts.

"Do you understand that you will have a different last name and that the Hatts will be your new family?"

Such a strange word, *family.* Maybe they didn't understand its meaning either.

I answered, "Yes, sir," to each of his questions. After a half hour of interrogation, I left with my new "family." We drove home in silence.

I didn't want any of them to see me cry, but inside, I was sobbing. I missed my brother and sister so much, and the flame of that hope had been fuel then suppressed, leaving me desiring them still more.

Something changed inside me that day. I had to accept I was helpless and alone and hope that someone else would sing Tawny her favorite song at bedtime, and someone besides me would put my little brother to bed and rub his belly because he had stomach aches at night. I wondered how a heart could ache that badly.

The day I thought I could be a good big sister to Dana seemed so long ago, leaving me wondering what my purpose was now with no one to protect and look out for? There was nothing left for me in this miserable hell on earth.

CHAPTER THIRTEEN

Lost Treasure

FOSTER KIDS usually are a lot smarter than they're given credit for. Not without reason. We have heard, seen, and experienced more than most biological children do in their lifetime. Our souls age faster than our physical development, so we long for what we have missed—to be loved by our adoptive parents in the same way they love their biological children.

We would like to be treated equally and have the same things: new clothes, bathroom necessities, and shoes as our other siblings. We don't want to feel like a stranger in their house or have to ask to enter a room. We want to go on a vacation without having to get it cleared with caseworkers and biological parents who are not even raising us. We hope the people at the place we're staying value us and want us to be with them because we're part of their family. We want them to like us.

We hope they try to understand us and our sometimes strange world we live in. If we're hanging onto things that look like trash, it may be that we're holding onto the only memories of our past we have left. And we do hold on to them. Sometimes forever. For me, it was empty packages of Funyans and chocolate milk. I know they might have been trash in other people's worlds, but in mine, that trash was my treasures, my beautiful last memory with my dad. After he left that night, I washed out the chocolate milk container and let it dry then cleaned out the crumbs and grease that had settled in the Funyuns bag. Then I put them in my "trash" bag alongside the Clue game, my *Black Beauty* book, and the Holly Hobbie doll my mother had given me. These were not just treasures, they were evidence of a different age and time. They were priceless relics of a lost world.

They gave me three drawers in Dana's room. I used the top drawer for my underwear, bras, and socks. The middle drawer for shorts and jeans, and the bottom drawer for my treasures. It was the first real dresser I had ever had, even if I was sharing.

Travis, my oldest adoptive brother, hated me from the first day I arrived at the Hatt's. He picked on me constantly and seemed jealous of my relationship with Kent even though, as far as I saw, he never made an effort to be with him.

I thought Travis was lazy and dumb, and it seemed to me that he was always miserable. Shortly after I moved in, he made up this poem about me.

Celeste is a dope.
She ate a bar of soap.
Bubbles here and bubbles there.
Bubbles in her underwear.

He was a bully and was always hurting people and animals. He liked camping alone in the woods, which I thought was strange. I couldn't imagine anything good happened on those trips.

One day, I went to my drawer of treasures to find everything gone. I stared at the empty drawer searching the corners as if I just looked harder, my treasures would reappear. But they didn't. The only thing in the drawer was a piece of lined paper with the poem Travis scrawled on it.

Celeste is a dope.
She ate a bar of soap.
Bubbles here and bubbles there.
Bubbles in her underwear.

I had already guessed he had taken my things, but the note was proof. I fell onto my knees, and again, hopelessness engulfed me. I would never see my beloved treasures again. There was nothing left to prove that anyone had ever loved me.

The only things left of my existence were two pieces of paper: a birth certificate with the name Celeste Lynn Hatt and the stupid poem. I hated them both.

CHAPTER FOURTEEN

Does This Mean Eternal Hell?

KENT AND KATHY were about to try another way to save their marriage. They decided to be "sealed" in a Mormon temple. This meant they would participate in a temple ceremony that would bind their marriage and family together for eternity. They were members of the Mormon church, the predominant religion in Utah, and they believed that if we were sealed forever in heaven, things would be better on earth. I was confused by the word sealed, which later turned for me, into a literal fear of God.

We entered the white alabaster temple in South Jordan, Utah. The interior was also all white, and I remember being struck by the beauty of the building. They took us children into an area where we could change into special white clothes, watch a movie about Mormonism, and eat snacks.

Even there, in the "House of God," I was told how lucky I was to have such a loving family that would want

me sealed to them for time and all *eternity. Eternity?* I pan-
icked. You mean there was no escaping Kathy even after
I died? That felt like a sentence to hell. I had held to the
belief that, as an adult or in death, I could have a happily
ever after. Being placed with the Hatts by the state was one
thing. But being placed with the Hatts *by God for eternity*
was beyond comprehension.

Dressed in all white, we went into another room filled
with church members and friends who were there to wit-
ness the sealing. Everyone was also dressed in white with
peculiar hats and veils on their heads. I thought the men's
hats looked like chef hats.

The guests sat on chairs on both sides of the room. In
the center of the room was an altar. The six of us kneeled
around it with Kathy to my left. When the officiator
asked us to take hands, Kathy barely touched mine. Just
her touch caused a dark chill to run through my body. I
was only nine years old then, and I don't remember much
about the ceremony except for the words "families are forever" and Kathy's kiss.

After the ceremony ended, Kent and Kathy were invited
to kiss their children. I remember wondering how Kathy
would pull this off in front of an entire group of people.
Kathy first leaned to her left, lovingly smiled, and kissed
Dana's cheek. Then she turned to me, looked directly into
my eyes with obvious hatred, leaned toward me quickly,
and barely touched my cheek with her lips. Afterward, I
suspect she would have spit into a spittoon if one had been

provided. I didn't care about the kiss. The only thing I could think about was the sentence of *time and all eternity.*

Then things got worse. Not long after the temple sealing, Kent had a massive heart attack. He had worked at Kennecott Copper Mine west of Salt Lake City in the Oquirrh Mountains for more than a decade. After his heart attack, the doctors told Kent that he could no longer lift over fifteen pounds, meaning he could no longer work at the mine or on the farm.

The Hatts sold their farm in South Jordan, Utah. This provided the means to move to the southern Utah town of Cedar City so that Kent could start a new career to support the family. He enrolled in the college there to get his accounting degree.

Kathy's anger and frustration toward Kent and everything else she complained about increased. Not surprisingly, her abuse toward me intensified, as well.

Soon after we moved to Cedar City, Tawny and I became pen pals, and we began writing almost every day. Then, one day, I was told that Tawny and Austin would be coming to Cedar City for a visit. I was beyond excited.

Kathy was unhappy about them coming, but I hadn't seen my siblings since we moved, so she agreed. When they arrived, Kathy told them her house rules, which comprised them being confined to my room, with me, unless it was time to eat or bathe.

This was not received well by either sibling but mostly Austin. My little brother Austin was troubled. Being born an addict and nearly losing his life would create a path of hardship and heartache that not even he would fully understand. He was a cute, curious little guy who smiled and laughed a lot but struggled with authority. When Kathy asked him to come and eat dinner—since she was already unkind to him and he did not like her—he said he wanted to eat in my room. She replied, "Fine, just stay there."

Then, out of nowhere, she raged into my room and grabbed him. This wasn't hard for her as he was a sickly boy, and she was a very large woman. She threw him into the bathtub with his clothes on and turned on the cold water. Immediately, the freezing cold water poured over him as he huddled into a ball and cried. I ran to the bathroom screaming at Kathy. She slammed me violently into the door then yelled at me that this is what happens when children don't obey. I went back again, only to be shoved into the door a second time.

Over and over, Kathy repeated this until she was too tired to continue abusing us. She turned off the shower and walked away, mumbling that we had to *clean up the mess* we created.

I quickly helped Austin get undressed, dried him off, and changed him into his pajamas. I wrapped him in a blanket, and we sat over the heater vent while I held him as he shivered. I never asked them to come back. There was no way I would allow that experience, or worse, to happen again.

CHAPTER FIFTEEN

A Bully and A Liar

THERE IS ONE PART OF MY STORY which has particularly weighed heavily on my heart for thirty-eight years.

Through all I went through, I had become a bully and a liar. I needed to admit this. After all these years, I needed to finally own it. I cannot recall a more shameful time in my life, but being authentic isn't just about sharing how you were hurt but also the pain you may have caused others.

I was in seventh grade during the time this happened. At this time in my life with the Hatts, I wanted Kathy to love and accept me as her kid. But it was like waiting for a bus at a stop that no longer existed. As the pain of rejection became more significant, my need to fit in with others became more important than anything. I didn't care who I hurt. Even those who did nothing but be kind to me.

I cruelly hurt my friend Jennifer. She wouldn't be the first Jennifer to enter my life, but she is the most memorable.

One might say that she was overweight, but in reality, she was just bigger than my skinny ass. She was beautiful inside and out, with long brown hair and beautiful brown eyes. She had friended me the moment I started junior high school. Maybe she just recognized that I needed love and a friend.

We hung out at school, mostly during lunch since I was not allowed to see friends outside of school unless Dana was with me. I had reached a point where I would rather not have friends than put them through the misery of Dana and the Hatt family.

The cafeteria was a large room where everyone could see each other. It had big round tables with ten chairs surrounding each one. It was a time to get to know other kids, but I didn't have that kind of courage. But Jennifer was kind and good, so I sat with her.

I hadn't been there long when I noticed a particular group of popular girls at school. I had never seen their type. They seemed to be perfect. Perfect hair. Perfect clothes. Perfect lives. Everyone wanted to be around them. The five perfect girls walked through the halls without a care in the world. *How cool,* I thought, *would it be to be one of them?* I even had a name for their group; the *Famous* Five. I wanted to be one of them. I wanted to be admired for my beauty and be accepted everywhere I went.

I began to look at Jennifer more closely. No one seemed to know her, like her, or even notice her. One day, I decided I didn't want to be like her. As I looked at the popular girls, I suddenly felt embarrassed to be with Jennifer.

This was not my only betrayal. Looking back at that time, I see more clearly my need for attention and validation at any cost.

Things were always strange at the Hatt house, but one day was particularly unusual. Kent and Kathy had been fighting again, but this time, Kathy did something incredibly extreme, even for her. She asked Kent why he had hit me.

Then she turned and asked me to tell her about what happened. I was so confused. Kent hadn't hit me. He had never even yelled at me. Why did she want me to say he had? I asked her what she was talking about.

She said again, but even more sternly, "Tell us what happened, Celeste. What did Kent do to you?" She smiled at me for the first time in the almost four years I had lived there.

None of this made sense, but I had a strong impression I had better come up with something. So I did.

"He grabbed me by the back of my hair and yelled at me to finish the dishes."

It surprised me I could come up with a lie so quickly, but Kathy smiled at me ,again. I loved having her smile at me. It wasn't love, of course, it was her sick game. I didn't even care. She seemed to like me for the first time, and I ate it up like a rat eats D-con. By now, my siblings had heard the fighting and ran into the room to see what was happening. I'd never had all of their attention before either, and it felt great.

Even Travis smiled then asked his dad with unabashed excitement, "You pulled her hair?"

It wasn't that Kent didn't punish the other kids—he did, especially the boys. They were disrespectful, spoiled, and talked back regularly, so he would give them an occasional "kick in the ass" as he referred to it, or twist their ears.

I never did anything to deserve his anger, and the other kids resented me for it. But now, for the first time, I seemed to have their respect if not their admiration. So, I kept going, fabricating a story about Kent pulling my hair and yelling at me, the whole time watching him look at me in bewilderment.

Then tears slowly welled up in the kind man's eyes, and he said, "I forgive you for what you're doing, Celeste. I understand."

He did not fight back, to Kathy or me, but just quietly walked away, defeated more by my attack than Kathy's. I had betrayed him, the only one in the family that was ever kind to me.

The next day in school, my heart was so sad. Not just for the lies I said about Kent but for hurting one of the only men in my life that had never hurt me. I would never have the chance to say I was sorry or to even have a conversation with Kent again as he passed away from a heart attack just a few months later.

The next day, I saw Jennifer as I arrived at school. Almost immediately, my sadness turned to anger. Jennifer reminded me of not being seen or being heard. I didn't say "hi" or even acknowledge her. Later, I didn't sit with her at lunch. That afternoon, she caught up with me in the hall and asked if I was okay.

"I'm fine," I snapped and walked away. I didn't even look at her.

After school, I saw the famous five standing by their lockers.

"Hey, new girl," one of them shouted.

I turned around to see them all looking at me.

"Come here," she commanded.

I walked over to them. I couldn't believe they were talking to me. I tried to be cool. "Yeah?"

"Why do you hang out with that fat girl at lunch?"

"Jennifer?"

"Yeah, Tubby Jennifer," she said. All the girls laughed.

"I don't really like her," I said. "She's just the only person I know at this school."

Even then, I couldn't believe what I was saying. None of the other girls said anything as they followed the first girl's lead, who directed everyone like an army drill sergeant.

The girl shrugged. "Well, you can hang out with us if you want."

"Really?"

The drill sergeant's eyes narrowed. "Sure, but we want you to help us teach Tubby Jennifer that she doesn't belong at this school. Only girls like us should go here."

Girls like us. Did they just include me in their ranks? No way. This was the best day ever!

"What do you want me to do?" I said unctuously.

"We'll tell you tomorrow. Just meet us here before school starts."

I was excited. "Okay, see you tomorrow."

That was the best walk home from school in my whole life. Any thought of right and wrong was buried beneath my desire to be with these girls—to be someone special. I'd forgotten, or chose to forget, how it felt to be hurt. I could only think of being accepted, and this was my chance.

On my way to school the next day, I was excited imagining meeting up with the cool girls. Now was my chance to prove my worth. Whatever they asked, I knew I was up to the task.

The girls were waiting for me when I walked through the school's side doors. They welcomed me with broad smiles to their little clan.

I've arrived! I thought. I felt so important. I finally had cool friends.

The drill sergeant gave me a curt nod. "When Tubby Jennifer gets here, go over and talk to her."

"Why?"

She didn't let me finish. "Just do it."

While we waited for Jennifer to arrive, the girls talked and laughed at everything the drill sergeant said. I smiled, laughed, and joined in like I was a part of the cool group, but I had no idea what they were talking about.

Then Jennifer walked in.

"Go hang out with her," the drill sergeant commanded.

I did what she said. I tried to look cool as I walked over to Jennifer. "Hi."

Jennifer opened her locker, reached for some books, and then looked at me. "Hi back. New friends?"

"Oh them," I said casually. I was about to continue, but the girls suddenly were beside us. The drill sergeant slammed Jennifer's locker shut in her face. Then she said to me, "Hey, new girl, did you tell her what you nicknamed her?"

I was puzzled. "What?"

"Yeah, the name you call her. The one you told us yesterday."

"Tubby Jennifer?" I said. It was a question, not a statement.

"Yeah, that's the one," she laughed. "Jennifer, what do you think of the nickname your friend gave you?"

Jennifer looked at me with bewilderment and hurt in her eyes. Her face turned bright red. I suddenly felt sick. I wanted to say that I wasn't the one who came up with the name, but, to my shame, I didn't say anything. Jennifer just ran down the hall. The girls laughed, and we all walked away as if the interaction was normal.

From that day forward, I would no longer hang out with Jennifer. I stayed with the drill sergeant, and like her friends, I laughed at her ridiculous nothingness and reassured her how amazing she was. I was a puppet.

Truthfully, I missed Jennifer, but I loved being known and noticed even more. For weeks, every interaction with Jennifer was negative. Any place we saw her, the drill sergeant would call out her new name, Tubby Jennifer, and we would all laugh. Drill sergeant would tell her she was fat and not welcome at this school—that only skinny, pretty girls could attend, and she was neither.

It seemed like every time Jennifer came around a corner, the famous six were there. At lunch, we would sit at the table next to where she sat. The drill sergeant would taunt her, tease her, and do everything she could to make her feel small and miserable.

One day in the lunchroom, drill sergeant told Jennifer that she could sit with us if she stood on the table. To my surprise, Jennifer obeyed. Standing on the table, with everyone looking at her, the drill sergeant threw a sandwich at her and told her to eat it, so she could get fatter.

Everyone laughed as Jennifer got off the table and ran out of the cafeteria. Even though the rest of us in the cool group didn't do anything to Jennifer, at least directly, we were all just as guilty as we stood by and watched her be humiliated by a mean girl. But I was more guilty than the others; I did not defend my beautiful friend.

Jennifer wasn't at school one day, and I assumed she was sick. But after a few days of not seeing her, I asked one of her teachers if they knew where she was. The teacher said that Jennifer had transferred schools. I wondered if the famous five would still allow me in their group. That's all I was concerned about.

Then the Hatts moved again. I never got to find out.

CHAPTER SIXTEEN

A Demon's Choice

THE DAY I LEARNED that Jennifer had transferred, I came home to find Kathy waiting for me.

I walked into the house to see the others gathered in the living room. Kathy told us kids we needed to choose who we wanted to live with. She said she was leaving Kent and moving to Big River, California. She said her things were already in the car, and we would live with her sister, our Aunt Pat.

I was speechless. Kathy stared at me with a piercing look that could poke a hole into my heart. In a threatening tone, she asked my decision. I wanted to stay with Kent and to tell him I was sorry for betraying him. I wanted to stay with him and make everything right. But what would I say after what I did to him? Weeks had gone by, and we had yet to speak. Why would he want me to stay? I packed up my garbage bag, and we left.

The Hatt's temple "sealing" did not save their marriage, and it wasn't long before they were divorced. We were not allowed to see Kent or have any relationship with him. As far as Kathy was concerned, he was already dead.

We didn't stay in Big River very long. Soon, Kathy moved us back to Utah to a suburb of Salt Lake City called Kearns where I attended Kearns Junior High School. I was in the eighth grade when Kent passed away.

I don't recall crying at all when I was told he had died or even at his funeral. But when I think of him now, my eyes fill with tears that our last interaction was of me lying to Kathy about him abusing me. I wish I could thank him for the years he was kind to me and taught me a work ethic that would carry me through the rest of my life. I wish.

Kearns Junior High had a group of girls that reminded me of the mean girls at the drug rehabilitation center in Michigan. They were constantly picking on me and telling me they wanted to beat me up. They weren't considered popular or pretty, like the famous five, they were just bullies.

Shortly after Kent's passing, these girls approached me in the hallway determined to cause trouble. I'd finally had enough and told them to meet me at the corner of the school farthest away from the building. I told them I would fight all three of them.

It's strange how things randomly circle back in your mind, and this was one of those times. After school ended, I was heading out to meet the girls and thought of the bar- bie dolls and beating that girl so badly that she was taken to the hospital. I remembered the notoriety that experience gave me with the other kids.

As I approached the girls, about forty kids had gathered around to watch. A girl fight always seemed more interesting than a boy fight to kids my age. I knew I needed weapons, so I grabbed rocks that were large enough to hit someone. I did not wait for them. I immediately started swinging, and the cheers from the crowd motivated me.

Eventually, the three would win by the power of sheer numbers, and I was on the ground holding my head while all three of them kicked me. I glanced over and saw one of the rocks I had dropped. I picked it up and hit one of the girls on the side of her head as hard as I could. It seemed like slow motion as I watched her spin and land motionless on the ground, blood pouring from her head.

The crowd instantly stopped cheering, and there was dead silence. I looked down at the girl and immediately remembered what had happened in Michigan; I could attack her while she was down. But I was not eight anymore. I was twelve, and I knew that it was wrong.

I thought of Jennifer in Cedar City and how I had hurt her to the point she left the school. This was not who I wanted to be. Defending myself was one thing, but knowingly inflicting pain on someone was another. I started to run. I did not look back.

I had bruises on my body from being kicked, but I did not have any marks on my face, so no one noticed at home. That next Monday when I returned to school, I was prepared to be pulled into the office, but no one ever called. Pecularly, no one ever reported me. The mean girls never bullied me again.

A couple of days later, I was walking down the hall during class change when I saw her. Her hair was not long anymore, but it was definitely her. Jennifer from Cedar City. My heart froze. This was my chance to make it right and apologize to her for what I had done.

As I started toward her, I'll never forget the look of horror on her face. She just stared at me in disbelief. I can only imagine what she must have been thinking. She had changed schools, moved three hours away, and landed in the exact same school as me. I called her name and was ready to beg for forgiveness, but she ran off, and I never saw her again. To this day, I would give anything to see her and, with all my heart, apologize.

CHAPTER SEVENTEEN

Kathy's Wrath and Lying Counselors

WITHIN WEEKS, we moved to West Valley City and another junior high school. Our lives were a whirlwind of events that made Kathy even angrier and meaner than ever. She developed severe health issues, and her verbal abuse escalated to physical abuse.

I attempted to run away once to a friend's house, but the family got understandably nervous about harboring a minor and made me return home. Kathy was furious with embarrassment and threw me into a wall, knocking me unconscious.

I remember waking up laying on the couch with a cold washcloth on my forehead, and Dana yelling, "You've killed her. You've killed her!"

I looked up to see Kathy on the phone. I could hear her making one call after the other to family telling them there had been an accident, that I was running through the house and fell into a wall. I never told anyone the truth. I knew better since the last time I told an adoptive aunt about the abuse, it only worsened the situation. In her state of mind, I feared she might kill me.

Kathy's health continued deteriorating as her diabetes worsened. I thought me helping more around the house would make her love me or at least not hate me so much, so I took babysitting jobs to help buy groceries. Since I couldn't drive, I carried heavy bags for several miles to and from the store regardless of the weather.

Still, nothing changed. As Kathy's abuse increased, I noticed a shift within myself. I was beginning to think of ways to end Kathy's life. I was having horrible thoughts and plotting ways for Kathy to die, so she could no longer hurt me. It was either take her life or lose my own. Frankly, either were fine. I was not in a good place and didn't know where to turn.

Kathy used her church as a weapon. One time the LDS (Mormon) Social Services department of the church arranged counseling for Kathy and me. Kathy had told them I was a troubled teenager and believed I had been the root of her and Kent's marital problems, forcing them to divorce—something the Mormon church does not take lightly.

Kathy and I went to the counseling center and met with a therapist who gave us some suggestions that might help our relationship. I thought it was odd the therapist never wanted to talk to me alone. She allowed Kathy to tell her how difficult it was to raise such a troubled child. All I could do was listen. I was never provided the opportunity to tell her about the abuse or cruelty I had suffered.

One visit, out of nowhere, the therapist asked, "Would you like to see your biological mother?"

"I was told that was impossible," I said.

"I think I can make that happen. That is, if your mother *wants* to see you."

"Yes," I said eagerly. "I want to ask her if she's doing better."

The therapist leaned back in her chair. "I'll see what I can do. We'll meet again in two weeks."

Those were two very long weeks. I was excited to start again with my mom and for the chance to be a better daughter. I thought of what I would do differently, and I wondered whether she would feel the same. I thought if she and I could reunite, then we could at least have visitation rights to see Tawny and Austin. I made up a whole happily ever after in my head during those two weeks.

It was a Wednesday afternoon when we went back to the therapist. On the drive there, Kathy said, "I doubt your mom will want to see you. She has probably moved on with her life and forgotten all about you."

Her remarks were like a stab to my heart.

I sat before the therapist, and she asked us how the past two weeks had been.

Kathy started to answer, "Okay…"

I quickly interjected, "Did you get a hold of my mom? Does she want to see me?"

Kathy rolled her eyes and briefly nodded at the therapist as though giving her permission to proceed. Looking back, it was obvious the two of them had already spoken about their plan to help me settle into my environment by ripping the hope out of me.

"I did reach out to your mom," the therapist said. "She is no longer in New York, but she has no interest in seeing you."

My heart froze. "Are you sure you talked to the right mom?" I asked. "Maybe you made a mistake."

"I didn't make a mistake, Celeste. I'm sorry." She didn't sound at all sorry to me.

Later in my life, I reached out to my adoption agency and learned that in "closed" adoptions, seeing my biological mother would have never been an option, and the therapist must have used this as a tactic to see what reaction she could get out of me. I couldn't imagine someone, a professional counselor no less, being so cruel. She was supposed to help people not break them. I cried for days.

As this was a church sponsored organization, I felt even more abandoned by God. Wasn't He supposed to have good, honest people helping his children?

CHAPTER EIGHTEEN

Cinderella

IT WAS IN WEST VALLEY CITY, another suburb of Salt Lake City, that I met Lisa. She was a breath of fresh air. Although a year younger than me, to me she represented freedom.

Our connection was immediate. It was also damaging. She took me to wild parties, and for the first time, I was introduced to drugs and alcohol. You would think since my biological parents were drug addicts, I would have had this chance before, but I didn't. And neither drugs nor alcohol were available to me at the Hatt's. Mormons weren't supposed to use drugs or drink alcohol. But, apparently, for Kathy at least, abusing children was okay.

Lisa's mom worked two jobs, so Lisa and I would skip school and go to her house at least a couple times a week. We would have friends over, eat, and hang out all day. Lisa had an older sister named Sylvia. Unlike Lisa, Sylvia was a "good girl." She was responsible and never missed school. So Lisa and I had the house to ourselves.

Lisa had more worldly experience than I did in just about everything. She knew how to use her looks and sexuality to get what she wanted which is why boys were always giving us alcohol and inviting us to parties. I had never had so much fun or felt so free in all my life.

Lisa also made me feel safe as she became my protector. At parties, after I had drank too much, she would literally find a room and "tuck me into bed." I would hear her outside of the bedroom telling everyone that if they touched me, she would kick their ass, and everyone knew that was exactly what she would do.

The boys all liked Lisa, and other girls were always out to get her for stealing their boyfriends. She just said she didn't understand why the girls would be mad at her for their boyfriends cheating. But at parties, girls were always confronting her. She learned to defend herself and became more and more violent, especially when she drank. But Lisa was always loyal to me. She was always there for me when I needed help or a place to land.

Kathy may have been sick, but she was healthy enough to keep up on her mind games. The week of my ninth-grade promotion, the moms of my group of friends pitched in to give us a fun graduation experience. They had rented a limo and stocked it with fake champagne (sparkling cider of course) and glasses engraved with each of our names. The entire group was planning on getting ready at a friend's house to do our hair and makeup together.

The night before promotion, Kathy barged into my room and started rifling through my closet. She pulled out the beautiful red dress I'd bought for promotion.

"Where did you get the money to buy this dress?" she demanded.

"I bought it with my babysitting money," I said.

"And who took you to the store to buy it?"

I chose my words carefully. "Karen took me when I was babysitting. She paid me then asked if I wanted to get a dress." Karen was one of the young women leaders in our church. I often babysat for her and sometimes stayed for dinner with her family, allowing me to escape Kathy.

Kathy's jealousy took over, again. This time it was because of my friendship with Karen, who knew Kathy was no good. Kathy pulled my new dress off the hanger and ripped it, just like the evil stepmother in *Cinderella*. She screamed at me that a church dress was good enough for me to wear but then said, "You will not be going to promotion with those *slutty* girls."

When I told my girlfriends what she'd said, they were livid. They immediately began to plot ways to sneak me out so that I could go with them. They got another dress for me and were on a mission to rescue me. The plan might have worked, but Kathy locked me in a room in the basement the night of my ninth-grade promotion.

"Enjoy your evening alone," she said and closed the door, locking it with a padlock.

I was locked in there until she was sure the party was over, then she let me out. I spent the entire time plotting more ways to rid the world of this evil person and decided she was becoming weak enough that, eventually, I could hold a pillow over her face and smother her by holding it down with the weight of my body. I decided to get a job, so I could be away from Kathy as much as possible until the time came I would end her life.

Years later, I would learn about the severe abuse that, after I left, Kathy inflicted on Dana and Scott. I often wondered if my pillow idea would have really been the best solution for everyone.

CHAPTER NINETEEN

Flight of the Noodles

*I*N HIGH SCHOOL, the group of girls I hung out with loved to get into trouble. In spite of that, they were the best friends I had ever had. I had only known them for a year, but they made me happy, and I considered them family. For once, someone truly cared about me.

They also knew about the abuse I suffered at the hands of Kathy. One of the girls in the group was named Jennifer. She became my best friend.

Jennifer was braver than my other friends. She was the only one who ever came to my house and didn't care what Dana, or even Kathy, had to say about her being there. She was tall and had an intimidating presence. I think they were both afraid of her.

One afternoon Jennifer and I were downstairs in my bedroom—the small basement cell Kathy had sentenced me to in order to punish me for buying the promotion dress—

practicing for the upcoming dance club tryouts.

My new room was tiny, maybe ten by ten, with a bed and dresser on one side, so there wasn't much room for us to practice, but I had been grounded to the house, so it was all I had. Besides, Kathy didn't know I was trying out for the dance club and wouldn't have allowed it if she had.

The room had a single window which didn't have a screen since I had taken it off a few nights earlier to sneak out of the house. Suddenly, as Jennifer and I were practicing our routine, a pot of boiling noodles came flying in through the window, covering both of us in hot pasta. We looked up to see Travis and Dana running away from us.

We went to the bathroom to clean ourselves off. Tellingly, my main concern wasn't the burn caused by the hot water or my siblings hateful act, rather it was to clean up the noodles before Kathy saw them and punished me for the mess. I didn't know it would become a pivotal moment in my life.

It was after the noodle incident that Jennifer asked her parents if I could live with them. The two of us found a job we could work together, and I was excited to tell Kathy the good news. This new job would enable me to purchase more groceries than my babysitting job, so we thought that would be our best selling point.

At the time, one of Kathy's new games was the way I was allowed to communicate with her. I had two options. Option one was relaying everything through Dana. Option two was to talk to Kathy through her closed bedroom door.

Jennifer was with me and listened in disgust as I spoke to Kathy through the closed door about the great job opportunity I had and how I could help the family more.

Jennifer didn't say one word. She just stared at me in disbelief and mouthed the words, "W*hat the f---?*"

Afterward, we walked outside. Jennifer turned to face me. "You have to leave here."

"I can't," I said. "The last time I left, she knocked me out and told everyone in the family that I ran into a wall. She'll kill me."

Dana was standing there with us. "It's okay if you leave, Celeste. Mom doesn't want you here. She doesn't like you anyway."

Jennifer glared at Dana and said, "I talked to my mom, and she said it's okay if you live with us."

"I can't," I said again. "Kathy will hurt me. You have no idea."

Jennifer was now really upset. "Well then, I won't be your friend if you don't come with me. I can't just watch this bitch abuse you. I just can't. It's painful for me to watch, and it's unfair to you."

I'm not sure if Jennifer was serious about never being my friend or just trying to shake me into understanding how serious she was. Suddenly, she picked me up and threw me over her shoulder with me screaming and kicking.

"Put me down, Jennifer!"

"Just go, Celeste!" yelled Dana. "Mom won't even care. None of us will."

Dana's voice was like fingernails on a chalkboard. When Jennifer got me to the end of the street, she put me down. I turned around, staring at the house for several minutes. I looked around at all the neighbors on that street who I knew were aware of the abuse in our home but kept it a secret, even though I babysat most of their kids.

I decided right then it didn't matter what life I would have as long as it was not this one. I had just started tenth grade, and I was scared, but I committed to never go back to the Hatts. I would be homeless, if necessary, but I would never live with Kathy again.

Jennifer and I held hands as I walked away from the Hatts and that horrible life.

There are some amazing people who are not paid or sanctioned by the state to take children in but are simply willing to help. Jennifer's parents were that kind of people. They really couldn't afford another teenager and were not in a healthy marriage themselves, but they allowed me to stay with them, anyway.

Jennifer shared everything with me, her room, her clothes, her makeup, even her family. Jennifer literally saved my life. What I was willing to do to Kathy would have changed the trajectory of my life. I would have either ended up dead or killing Kathy and ending up a murderer.

One day, Kathy showed up at Jennifer's house with our church clergymen. I was so afraid of her I ran upstairs and locked myself in Jennifer's bedroom. The leader of the ward, the bishop, was at the door trying to convince me to come out and go home, telling me that home is where problems can be worked out.

"Celeste, will you come out and talk to me?" the bishop asked.

"I'm not coming out while Kathy is there."

"Celeste, God would want you to come out and talk to your mother."

"Kathy isn't my mom. Just ask her. She hates me. She will hurt me if I go back."

"Your mom won't hurt you, and she doesn't hate you," he said. "Or why would she be here? You know that the church can help with all of this. It can help you get back together with your family."

"She almost killed me the last time I tried to get away from her. Just ask her. She threw me into a wall and knocked me out. And I've already talked to your social services group. They wouldn't listen to me."

Now, Kathy spoke up, and she was mad. "If you don't come back with us now, I'll throw everything of yours out on the front lawn tomorrow. If you don't come and get it, I'll burn it all."

Kathy stormed out of Jennifer's house taking the clergymen with her.

The next day, Jennifer went with me to collect what we could from the Hatt's front lawn and left the rest. I guess she burned my stuff. I never found out.

After all I'd been through, I was emotionally broken. I started drinking alcohol and missing a lot of school. I was put into a night school program and eventually dropped out altogether. I lost faith in all churches and their gods. I did not believe that churches, or at least Kathy's, had my best interest in mind, only their own. And if there was a God, I didn't believe that He loved me.

I'm not sure if I became too overwhelming for Jennifer's parents, or if they just had too much going on in their own family—perhaps a bit of both—but after several months, they kindly told me I would need to find another living arrangement.

The only thing I could think of was to ask a married cousin in Arizona who I had become close to, if I could live with her. She agreed, and Jennifer's dad drove me all the way to Lake Havasu, Arizona, where he dropped me off at my cousin's home.

Lake Havasu, Arizona, was an interesting place. My cousin's family was financially broke, but the town had a lot of money. It was the first time I had met people with money to lose. And it seemed that drugs were everywhere.

I dabbled with drugs, but growing up with my parents' addictions made me nervous about doing too much. I was, however, willing to drink excessive amounts of alcohol. I liked the feeling of being numb and not having to think. Alcohol helped me, at least temporarily, to feel no pain.

I didn't consider the risks or the ramifications of the situations I was putting myself in. I was making one poor decision after another, and before long, I woke up more than a few times with no idea where I was or how I got there.

I was heading down a dangerous path, and I didn't care.

After a few short months, my cousin told me they were moving to Riverside, California. We took a road trip to visit, and I knew that place would not be for me. We would only be forty-five minutes from Los Angeles, which could be a recipe for disaster with my current emotional and rebellious nature.

It was at this time that I met my third Jennifer. Her life was completely opposite of my cousin's. Polar opposites, to be exact. Jennifer's family had money. A lot of money. Her parents were divorced but owned the largest construction company in the valley. She asked her mom if I could live with them, and she said yes.

Their house was twenty-three thousand square feet with two separate wings and outbuildings. With six bathrooms and five bedrooms, their home had won several awards and was listed in magazines as the Best Place to Live in Lake Havasu.

But their money was not the greatest blessing to me; it was Jennifer's mom, Irene, and how she lived her life—disciplined in everything. The way she ate, how she dressed, her exercise routine, and how she carried herself inspired me. Despite the challenges of her divorce and being a single mom, she was a woman to be admired and respected. Beautiful inside and out, she was the first to tell me I could be much more than I allowed myself to be. She said to live with her, I was not to miss a day of school, and she would ensure I had everything I needed and opportunities to succeed.

Up to that point, the women I had been around for most of my life drank and smoked too much, and put their needs ahead of their children's. They didn't care for their bodies and let people use them.

I was drawn to Irene's energy, love, and light; I wanted to be like her. However, history repeated itself, and within a few months of living with Jennifer and her mom, Irene explained that she needed to get her daughter into a mental health program. I wasn't surprised. I knew that Jennifer suffered with deep depression, too serious to be helped at home.

Irene felt terrible. She told me she would take me anywhere I wanted to go, but I couldn't stay there. So again, I packed up my garbage bag (yes, I still had it), climbed into the biggest Winnebago I had ever seen, and drove back to Utah. Just weeks before Thanksgiving, they dropped me off at another house where I had been before—my friend Lisa's house.

Irene handed me seven hundred and fifty dollars cash in an envelope, gave me a big hug, and reminded me that I could live the life I chose. Then, with tears in her eyes, she wished me good luck, got back in the Winnebago, and drove away. In my heart, I hoped that I could someday be just like her.

CHAPTER TWENTY

Home is Where They Have to Keep You

M<small>Y FRIEND</small> L<small>ISA</small> lived here with her sister, Sylvia, and their mother Carlie. Carlie didn't need another teenager to raise, but when I called Lisa, she told me to come, so I did. The truth is, I didn't have anywhere else to go. What I've learned from Carlie since then is that Lisa had only asked if I could stay for the weekend.

When Irene dropped me off, Sylvia walked out to the front yard with her arms folded. She glared at me as the motorhome drove away.

"What are you doing here?" she asked.

I didn't say anything. I just walked toward the front door.

Sylvia stared me up and down as I walked past her into the house. Apparently, no one had told her I was coming, and she was not happy. I don't blame her. All she remembered of me was catching me with Lisa stealing her mom's car. To Sylvia, I was bad news. She didn't know that I didn't want to be bad news. The truth is, she didn't know me at all.

Sylvia was two years older than me. She was popular, a cheerleader, in the dance company, and got good grades. From her perspective, I was just a troublemaker and would make problems for her sister and family.

The next few months were awkward, and I avoided Sylvia when possible, which wasn't easy in a three-bed-room house. But gradually, her distrust and anger began to diminish, and, over time, Sylvia and I became friends. She was a positive role model, and, like Irene, I wanted to be like her. Today, I am happy to call her sister and one of my best friends. I respect her immensely.

It only took two months of living there before Lisa went to her mom and asked, "Do we have to keep her?"

Sharing a twin bed and borrowing her clothes was finally wearing on her. The honeymoon was over.

I was doing dishes one night when Carlie came into the kitchen and asked to speak to me.

Here it comes, I thought.

I closed the dishwasher and turned to look at her. Mentally, I started packing.

"What are you doing?" she asked.

"The dishes..."

What Carlie said caught me off guard. "You know, Celeste, you don't have to be perfect to live here."

I laughed nervously. "Of course, I do."

"No," she said seriously. "*Home* is where they have to keep you."

I had never heard that before. I thought she was teasing me. "What does that even mean?"

"It means you cannot get kicked out just because you make a mistake. You can live here, Celeste. This is your home."

I was so surprised that I'm not sure I even said thank you.

"But," she added. "I have one rule."

I wasn't sure what to expect. "What's that?"

She looked me straight in the eyes. "You have to get your ass back in school."

I grinned. "No problem."

"I'm serious," Carlie said. "This is not an option."

Before now, only Irene had ever cared whether I attended school, and I figured if it was a requirement to have a place to live, then why not? But this time was different. This time I wanted to go. I wanted more from my life.

The process of getting back into school required an unbelievably grueling amount of work. But having people around me willing to help and support was something I had never experienced. I worked hard because they had put their faith in me, and I didn't want to let them down.

Unfortunately, my connection to the Hatts wasn't over. Kathy found out where I lived and would not leave me alone. She called my school and told the principal I was a bad kid and should be locked up or sent back to child welfare. He tried to explain to Kathy I was doing remarkably well, and he could see no reason to turn me into the state. Still, Kathy was her typical relentless self.

Fortunately, the principal was one of my most stalwart supporters. He would stop me in the hall, point to his watch, and say, "Don't be late, Celeste. Don't give her an excuse." He also encouraged me to try out for the drill team, so that I had a "fun" reason to be at school.

Kathy only stopped calling after Carlie threatened to turn her in to the police for cashing my social security checks. My days of dealing with Kathy had finally come to an end, except for going there to pick up the monthly social security check I received after Kent's passing.

My girlfriends and I had a routine of picking up my check, then going from Kathy's house to the local Smith's grocery store to cash it. That's where I met Carlos, who would end up being my first husband and my children's father.

Tammy, one of my girlfriends, knew Carlos because they went to the same junior high school. One day, he asked Tammy for my phone number. I told her I thought he was cute. That was code for *he can have my phone number*.

The next day, he called me, and we hung out every day after that. He was three years my senior, and, like Carlie, expected me to go to school. If I spent the night at his place on a school night, he would drop me off at 6 a.m. for drill team.

Carlos was the first guy I'd ever felt completely safe with, and I was head over heels. I could not imagine ever being with anyone else. One week after high school graduation, I would move in with him. Three years later, we would marry and have two children together.

Tammy was straight as an arrow. She didn't even lie. She was as perfect a girlfriend as I had ever had. She and I went to a department store once—she was eighteen, and I was seventeen— when I decided to steal some mascara. Tammy tried to talk me out of it by asking me why I wanted to do that. I just said, "Because I want to see if I can get away with it." So, I did, and the minute we stepped out of the store, security nabbed us. I was still a minor, but Tammy was an adult, and she paid dearly for my stupidity.

Carlie made me go before the judge, admit the whole scheme was my idea, and beg for forgiveness for Tammy. I had to attend court hearings, and Carlie ensured I got there. Horrifically, Kathy would be there, too. Fortunately, she was too afraid of Carlie to cause a stink.

True to Carlie's word, home was where they had to keep you. She also held me accountable to get my homework done, and when I eventually graduated from high school, Carlie was there to cheer for me—alongside the rest of my family and friends.

Tammy eventually forgave me, and we remain best friends to this day. Understandably, it took her parents a few more years than Tammy to forgive me.

I was the first person in my immediate family— including my biological parents—to graduate from high school. It was such a special day. I have a picture of me and the vice principal hugging at the podium, tears streaming down my face, as twenty people in the audience were screaming and cheering for me. I cherish that picture. I finally succeeded at something and felt a strong sense of pride in my accomplishment.

Carlie and my sisters, Lisa and Sylvia, were the first people in my life who did not give up on me. They were always there when I fell, ready to pick me up and provide a landing place to start again.

When I married Carlos, Carlie was there. By then, I had started calling her Mom. Soon after, she became grandma when my son was born. She is my children's favorite person in the world.

CHAPTER TWENTY-ONE

Back to the Courthouse

OR YEARS, the family joke was, I came for Thanksgiving and never left. On Thanksgiving and the ninth-year anniversary of my being dropped off on Carlie's front lawn, I gave a toast to all of them. I said this was the longest that I had ever lived with one family, and I just wanted to say thank you.

Carlie, my *mom* practically jumped out of her seat. "If that's how you feel," she said, "let's make it official."

"Make *what* official?" I asked.

"Let's adopt you."

I thought she was just having a sentimental moment because I honestly didn't think it was necessary. After all, I was married, and my kids already called her grandma.

"It's okay," I said. "You're my mom and my kid's grandma. All is well."

Out of nowhere, Carlie shared something that none of

us knew. She told us she had lost a child, and, when she met me, she felt I was the daughter she was supposed to have. The loss of her baby had been traumatic for Carlie. She was six months pregnant when she had to have an emergency abortion. Back then, there was no time allowed for grieving. Women were just expected to get on with their lifes. So, she went home to her three children.

How could I know what impact that would have on my life? There were other reasons to get adopted. Kathy was still my legal guardian, and the thought of something happening to me and her having any rights to my children terrified me. That February 1 was a perfect day for an adoption.

Fifty people crowded into the courtroom as my mother, Carlie, and I, stood before a judge in a beautiful new courthouse in downtown Salt Lake City.

I remember the judge had the biggest smile. He said he had never presided over an adult adoption before, and it made him happy. He suggested we each say something.

Carlie and I looked at each other, and I whispered to her, "What are you going to say?"

"I'm not sure," she whispered back.

I liken the moment to exchanging wedding vows. We turned and looked at each other, and she told the story again of losing a child and always knowing I was her daughter, and no one could ever take me from her.

I was filled with so much love, gratitude, and hope. I turned to the judge and said, "Seventeen years ago, I was in the building behind me at the county courthouse inside a judge's chambers. I was being told how lucky I was to be adopted. What that judge didn't know was he was sending me to an abusive home where I was never loved.

"Now, I'm standing in this beautiful new courthouse, facing forward, with that life behind me, and a beautiful future in front of me. A future that I chose. One that no one else chose for me. Today, I truly am lucky. Lucky to be adopted by a family that accepts me and reminds me every day I am unconditionally worthy of love and never, never asks me to leave."

Not the End

*T*HIS ISN'T THE END of my story. Not even close.

Before writing this book, I told myself and others I wasn't the same person I once was—as if I was ashamed of that child. But now, I know I am and will always be that little garbage bag girl. Today, I'm proud of her. She did something very difficult under the conditions she lived in; she survived.

Just recently, someone from my teenage years reached out to me; a man named Shane who had known me during those difficult times I lived with the Hatts. Shane and I visited some of our old haunts: Butterfield Canyon, the trailer park in Magna where we met, and our alma mater Cyprus High School. I suppose, in a way, it was like a war veteran returning to the now peaceful battlefield where he had once lived in terror. Shane was surprised when I told him I wanted to visit the old house where I'd lived with the Hatts.

"Are you sure that's a good idea?" he asked.

"No. But I won't know until I do."

So we went. The feelings I had seeing the Hatt home were immensely powerful. They made my stomach hurt. I knew I would never be back, so I began taking pictures of the house. As I did, I noticed a man across the street watching us from his front porch. After a few minutes, he took out his phone and began taking pictures of me. He walked over and took a picture of my car's license plate. Shane and I approached him.

"I'm sorry to worry you, sir," I said. "I used to live here."

The old man's brow furrowed. "I've lived here for more than fifteen years," he said. "I've never seen you."

"I was only fifteen when I lived here," I said. "That was more than thirty years ago."

He looked at me for a moment then said, "So you lived in the Vampire house."

"The *Vampire* house?"

"That's what we called it. There was such an evil spirit in that house that no one would buy it. It sat on the market for years. My son finally bought the place, but he had to pretty much tear everything out. Even the walls. Then he burned sage in there for days. Someone told him that sage has the power to remove evil spirits." The man looked at me intensely. "Did something evil happen there?"

"Almost every day," I said.

Shane and I walked back to my car. "You know you're safe now," he said.

"I know," I said softly.

"That was really courageous of you to go back," Shane said. "You're very brave."

"The girl who lived there was brave," I said. "She was a survivor."

The Hatt house today

Now that Tawny and I both have children, I have finally learned how to be her sister instead of her mother. We've reamined close ever since, helping each other raise our children the best we can.

Today, I'm the director of The Christmas Box International, an organization that provides shelters and care for abused, trafficked, and neglected children. Nearly every day, I see small versions of myself enter its halls: vulnerable, scared, hurt, and confused. I've had the privilege to be with those children, to hold and comfort them. In each of them, no matter their race or gender, I see myself.

Since we opened our doors more than twenty-seven years ago, no child has ever left our shelters with their belongings in a garbage bag. To some, it may seem like a small, if not symbolic, gesture. But I would venture these are people who have never carried their treasures from house to house in a garbage bag. Treasures as seemingly worthless and unimportant as me and thousands of other children.

I've heard it said the child is the mother to the adult. As I think about that scared, brave young woman who lived in the "vampire house," I realize that of all the women I have known, both good and bad, it is that little girl who is truly the mother of me. She made me. She endured the existential labor pains of a difficult life. She suffered every-thing, so I could be me. And for that, I am grateful to her.

And, despite the many years and experiences that have passed, she isn't gone. She never will be. But now, I have the maturity to fully embrace her. And even if she doesn't exist on paper records, she exists in my heart. I wouldn't be who I am today if it wasn't for her resilience, strength, and hope.

Today, I have three amazing children who know they are valued, loved, and safe. I have a beautiful, radiant grand-son I can't get enough of. Because of that little garbage bag girl, I have found real love and know its value. Most of all, because of her, after all she went through, the loss and pain and injustice, I have finally found my way home.

L. Celeste L. Edmunds. **R.** Tawny Hales

L. Celeste L. Edmunds. **R.** Tawny Hales

Keynotes, Seminars, Workshops and School Assemblies

Both Richard and Celeste are respected and effective communicators. As an acclaimed speaker, Evans has shared the podium with such notable personalities as President George W. Bush, President George and Barbara Bush, former British Prime Minister John Majors, Ron Howard, Deepak Chopra, Steve Allen, and Bob Hope.

To book Celeste Edmunds or Richard Paul Evans for a speaking engagement, please contact Diane Glad at diane@richardpaulevans.com or call (801) 870-3925. Thank you.

From Celeste L. Edmunds, Executive Director of
The Christmas Box International

Although the child welfare system failed me in many ways, I still believe that, in most cases, it was more the fault of the system than the people involved. As the director of The Christmas Box International, I've had the privilege of working with some of the most devoted and underappreciated advocates in the child welfare system. It is The Christmas Box International's mission to support our child welfare partnerships by providing opportunities and resources to help them in the difficult task of defending children.

Since 1996, The Christmas Box International has provided for and protected more than 145,000 children. We are proud of our record of serving children efficiently and effectively. I invite you to help us. To donate or to see how you can help please go to **www.thechristmasbox.org**.

Thank you.

Join the List

To join Celeste's mailing list, and for event
information, please visit Celeste's website:

CelesteEdmunds.com